Laozi
Tao t

Tao Te Ching

Books in the
SkyLight Illuminations Series

Tao Te Ching

Annotated & Explained

Translation and Annotation by Derek Lin

Foreword by Lama Surya Das

Walking Together, Finding the Way ®
SKYLIGHT PATHS®
PUBLISHING
Woodstock, Vermont

Tao Te Ching:
Annotated & Explained

2011 Quality Paperback Edition, Sixth Printing

Translation, annotation, and introductory material © 2006 by Derek Lin
Foreword © 2006 by Lama Surya Das

Library of Congress Cataloging-in-Publication Data
Lin, Derek, 1964–
Tao te ching : annotated & explained / by Derek Lin.
    p. cm.
Includes bibliographical references.
ISBN-13: 978-1-59473-204-1 (quality pbk.)
ISBN-10: 1-59473-204-3 (quality pbk.)
1. Laozi. Dao de jing. 2. Laozi. 3. Taoism. I. Title.

BL1900.L35L519 2006
299.5'1482—dc22
                                                    2006016008

10 9 8 7 6
Manufactured in the United States of America
Cover design: Walter C. Bumford III
Cover art: Lin Hsin Chieh

SkyLight Paths Publishing is creating a place where people of different spiritual traditions come together for challenge and inspiration, a place where we can help each other understand the mystery that lies at the heart of our existence.

SkyLight Paths sees both believers and seekers as a community that increasingly transcends traditional boundaries of religion and denomination—people wanting to learn from each other, *walking together, finding the way.*

SkyLight Paths, "Walking Together, Finding the Way," and colophon are trademarks of LongHill Partners, Inc., registered in the U.S. Patent and Trademark Office.

Walking Together, Finding the Way®
Published by SkyLight Paths Publishing
A Division of LongHill Partners, Inc.
Sunset Farm Offices, Route 4, P.O. Box 237
Woodstock, VT 05091
Tel: (802) 457-4000   Fax: (802) 457-4004
www.skylightpaths.com

Contents ☐

Foreword □

Lama Surya Das

The classic Tao Te Ching is, in my opinion, simply the wisest book ever written. I have read and reread it more than any other, and I have discovered that, unlike some of us, it only gets better and better with age. It reveals how both action and contemplation are paths to experiencing harmony, peace, and unity admidst diversity. It exemplifies both the Bodhisattva's skillful means of *being there* while getting there, every single step of the way, and the sublime secret that is the inseparability of oneness and noneness. It is also the ultimate primer on *menschkeit*, the art of living as a mature person of integrity, expounding how to be a good citizen and impeccable leader, attain genuine excellence, and realize self-mastery.

I first met the Tao Te Ching while in college in Buffalo, New York, during the tumultuous late 1960s. I was both enamored of the serene wisdom of this sublime text and mesmerized by its poetic brevity and tantalizing existential mystery. The morning after discovering the Tao Te Ching, I went straight to the bookstore and bought a copy, mulling over its cryptic verses day and night for weeks, finding it hard to go to class and endure academic lectures made pale by comparison. Over the years, some of my intrepid friends have even ventured to translate, or make versions of, the Tao Te Ching—a daunting task at best. As a Buddhist teacher, I often recommend the Tao Te Ching to my Dharma students to augment their spiritual studies and refine their sense of practice, of *presencing*.

My oldest Chinese friend in Hong Kong, the master puppet maker and old school Shanghai Zen man we called Michael Lee, used to read me one poem every morning at dawn, upstairs in his Kowloon slum apartment. When he died, he left me a hand-calligraphed copy of one of his ancient, yellowed rice-paper manuscripts of the Chinese classic, which remains one of my prized Asian artifacts. Derek Lin's fine new translation is as good as any and better than many, and his commentaries help illumine the text.

Word has it that one day some disciples found the elder Taoist philosopher Chuang Tzu in front of his house, sitting peacefully on the ground in the sun with his fresh-washed long hair cascading down around him. The students gathered around him and waited patiently. "What are you doing, Master?" they finally asked. "Drying my hair in the sun," the old sage replied. "Can we help you?" they wanted to know. "How can you help me; what is there that that needs to be done? My hair is being dried by the sun, and I am resting at the origin of all things."

This enigmatic story concerns the inner journey to the very center of things, beyond the dichotomy of doing and being and yet including both. The Taoist sages exemplify harmony and serenity, oneness, authenticity, and the spontaneous flow of naturalness. When nothing is done, nothing is left undone. That's really somethin', ain't it?

When I myself don't know what to do, which is surprisingly often, I try to take the Tao Te Ching's advice on the subject and do nothing, along the lines of the core Taoist notion of *wu wei*, which can be translated as "nonstriving." Overdoing things has produced so much more harm than good in this busy world; I think we'd do well to learn how to undo the habit of overdoing. The nineteenth-century enlightened vagabond and Tibetan Dzogchen master Patrul Rinpoche sums it up like this: "Beyond action and inaction the sublime Dharma is accomplished." This is the sublime peace of the Tao, something we can all experience by learning to live in the Tao through coming into accord with how things actually are—what Tibetan Buddhists call the natural state. Rather than trying to build skyscrapers to reach heaven and bridges to cross the raging river of samsara to reach the so-called other shore of nirvana, we could realize that it all flows right through us right now and there's nowhere to go, nothing to get, and all is perfect as it is. This deep inner knowing has a lot to do with trust and letting be; there is nirvanic peace in things just as they are.

This should not be misconstrued as a rationalization for mere quietism, cold indifference, passivity, or dropping out. Five hundred years before Jesus, Taoists taught passive resistance, a crucial element of world-changing modern spiritual activists such as Mahatma Gandhi, Martin Luther King Jr., and the Dalai Lama of Tibet. The ancient masters revealed how to be steadfast and supple, like water—flowing rather than fixed, rigid, or static—which is of great benefit, for water is stronger than even stone: water's constant flow will eventually wear anything down and carry everything away. Like the underlying continuum of reality, the great Tao is groundless and boundless; it is flowing, dynamic, yet unmoved amidst infinite change. "Yield and overcome, and you cannot be broken," they taught. "Bend and be straight." These are powerful words, truth spoken to power. Wisdom is as wisdom *does*. Awakening oneself awakens the whole world.

A little Tao goes a long way. The Tao Te Ching should be savored leaf by leaf, line by line, like haiku poetry—read and enjoyed, pondered, and reread again. These finely wrought, provocative, ultimate utterances are chock full of one-sentence sermons encapsulating universal wisdom in a charming, poetic form that leaves room for more interpretation than a Rorschach inkblot. Here we can find evocative pearls of wisdom concerning the mysteries of yin and yang and the manner in which the great Middle Way balances, harmonizes, and reconciles primordial dichotomies such as light and dark, heaven and earth, good and evil, man and woman, doing and being, life and death. These sublime little sutras have edified, instructed, encouraged, and entertained millions of people for millennia, and they continue to do so today. Like a veritable treasure trove, this masterful book of wise living and authentic being provides both spiritual sustenance and practical guidance, so necessary for us today and tomorrow.

The Tao Te Ching teaches that ruling an empire is like frying small fish. Think about that for a moment: Frying small fish takes a lot of care and trouble, yet is rewarded with little benefit. Studying the Tao Te Ching, however, is quite the opposite: Any effort invested in penetrating the subtle beauty and mystery of this ancient wisdom classic will be rewarded in abundance, as it has for generations.

> To see nothing is supreme seeing;
> to know nothing is supreme knowing.
> The great Way has no gate; this
> gateless gate invites entry.
> The Other Shore is not far:
> no oceans to cross,
> no within and without,
> no barriers, no wall, no hindrance.

Lama Surya Das
Dzogchen Center
Cambridge, Massachusetts

Introduction ☐

Some time ago, Amazon.com asked author Michael Crichton the follow-ing question: "If you were stranded on a desert island with only one book, which book would it be?"

His answer: the Tao Te Ching.[1]

Why? With millions of books from which to choose, including the greatest literature human civilization has ever produced, why the Tao Te Ching?

Crichton is not the only famous author with such a high regard for this ancient classic. Eckhart Tolle calls it one of the most profound spiritual books ever written.[2] What is it about the Tao Te Ching that inspires such praise? What accounts for its appeal?

The Tao Te Ching ranks with the Bible as one of the most translated books of all time.[3] This is all the more amazing when you consider that it achieves this status without the active promotion of religious institutions. Its widespread popularity throughout history is due to its own merits. Yet, at first glance, the Tao Te Ching may not seem very remarkable. It is a thin book; its eighty-one chapters are so concise that most of them do not fill an entire page. Somehow, its succinct words manage to convey a universe of wisdom and insight. Of all the great works of spirituality in human history, the Tao Te Ching may be the one that *says the most with the least*.

The richness of the Tao Te Ching invites—even demands—lifelong exploration. Its layers of meaning reveal themselves gradually. No matter how many times we study it, we discover something new with each read-ing. People who return to the Tao Te Ching after a hiatus often find that it seems like a completely different book. Even though its words remain the same, people change, and their additional life experience allows them to see new lessons that had been there all along but had gone unnoticed—lessons hidden in plain sight.

The Tao Te Ching presents its teachings without fanfare. Its author, Lao Tzu, does not claim divine inspiration, infallibility, or indeed any basis of authority. He is a mere philosopher, not a prophet or messiah. He does not ask us to accept anything on blind faith, but rather trusts that the lessons in the Tao Te Ching will prove themselves.

For these lessons are eminently practical. The Tao Te Ching is more than a commentary on spirituality; it is also a useful and down-to-earth guide to living life with grace, peace, and joy. Perhaps this, more than any other reason, is why the Tao Te Ching has cast its spell on generation after generation since its writing 2,500 years ago.

Birth of the Tao Te Ching

But just what is the Tao Te Ching? How was it written? And who exactly was its author, Lao Tzu? Taoist lore includes a legendary story about the origin of the Tao Te Ching that, like all good stories, reveals more than it first appears.

The events in the story took place during the decline of the Zhou Dynasty. The emperor had lost effective control, and noble families ruling individual states seized power, each hoping to consolidate China under its own rule. This was the precursor to the time of unrest in Chinese history known as the Warring States period.

> It was a typical day at the Hangu Pass, with no more than the usual number of people leaving or entering the Zhou State. Yin Xi [pronounced *Yin Shi*], the Commander of the Pass, looked over the travelers with watchful eyes. Recent news of impending war gave him ample reason to be especially alert.
>
> He saw an old man riding an ox and approaching slowly. Yin Xi sensed something different about this man. He trusted his intuition, so he walked up and asked, "What is your name?"

Unlike many Yin Xi had encountered before, the old man had a perfectly composed demeanor, neither pompous nor ingratiating. "I am Li Er," he replied.

The name was familiar. Yin Xi searched his memory and suddenly realized what his intuition was trying to tell him. "Are you not the one they call Lao Tzu, the Old Master?"

The old man's expression showed a flicker of reluctance, for he had no wish to draw attention. He nodded and answered, "Indeed."

"This is a great honor," Yin Xi said, bowing deeply. "I am an avid student of the Tao, and people say you teach the Tao with divine powers."

Lao Tzu smiled and said, "Let us not be too hasty in believing what people say, Commander."

"You must have tea with me before resuming your journey," Yin Xi said. "I absolutely insist." Lao Tzu saw the sincerity in Yin Xi's invitation and gladly accepted.

The Commander ordered his men to maintain vigilance and led Lao Tzu into his office. "Master, I am most curious about how you gained your legendary wisdom," Yin Xi said as he boiled water for tea.

"I claim no wisdom whatsoever. Others may get that impression only because I have served as King Wu's Royal Archivist over the years."

"Yes, it is said you won the position due to your ability to remember and summarize all the books you read. You must possess extraordinary knowledge," said Yin Xi.

"The Tao is about returning to simplicity, not pursuing knowledge. While there are certainly many books in the archives, by themselves they are powerless to capture the essence of the Tao."

"I find it difficult to imagine all those books in one place. Only a king can amass such a collection. I consider myself lucky to even see one book; a library is almost beyond my comprehension."

"Books are dead things, Commander," said Lao Tzu. "They contain the words of people long gone. The only way to gain living wisdom from dead books is by applying their words to life."

"True. Nevertheless, I suspect there are many scholars who desire your unlimited access to the books for themselves. Surely they wish to oust you in order to take over your position?" asked Yin Xi.

"Yes. The position may seem prestigious, but in fact it can be dangerous as well. Many people would use unscrupulous means, even violence, to take the position for themselves. Serving the king can also be dangerous—he has been known to execute his own advisors because they made some careless mistake."

"And yet you have survived and thrived as Royal Archivist for years. What is your secret?" Yin Xi asked eagerly as he poured tea into two cups.

"There is no secret. I use the Tao. Anyone can do the same thing—avoid danger and enjoy peace—through diligent cultivation of the Tao."

"In that case, you should be able to maintain your position for many years to come."

"No. My work for His Majesty is done," answered Lao Tzu. "I am able to retire. With the clouds of war hanging over the land, I see no reason to remain."

"How I envy your freedom! I hear about the impending war and think about going away myself, but I am tied to my property and career."

"Such is the nature of desires and attachments. That which you desire tends to bind you; relinquishing or reducing the desire tends to free you." Lao Tzu sat back and sipped his tea.

"It is a pity that you are leaving, Master, for I and many others can learn much from you," said Yin Xi. "Would you consider writing down some notes for us, so we can cultivate the Tao on our own?"

"That is an excellent idea," said Lao Tzu. "Let me write down the basic concepts, the standard sayings, and summaries of the major works in the Royal Archives. I will also include advice I have given King Wu over the years, for it too is based on the Tao."

"Would such advice apply to me, Master?"

"Certainly. The scope may change but the Tao remains constant no matter who you are. Royalty or commoner—it makes no difference to the Tao."

Lao Tzu began working. He leveraged his prodigious memory and understanding to create one concise chapter after another. Each chapter was a highly refined distillation of a major principle, a notable book, or a discussion with the king.

Finally, it was done. Lao Tzu gave Yin Xi the manuscript. Yin Xi could not believe it. What he held in his hands was King Wu's private library condensed into a compact form. He felt as if Lao Tzu had squeezed all the treasures in the royal vault into a diamond and handed it over to him.

Lao Tzu said his farewell, mounted the ox and continued on his way. Yin Xi called out after him, "Master! How can I thank you for this gift? Will I ever see you again?"

Lao Tzu smiled back at him and answered, "This gift is a dead thing, too. In that respect it is no different from other books. Remember: you can make it come alive by putting what it says into actual practice. When you do so, you will see me ... in the Tao."

Yin Xi looked on as Lao Tzu receded from view. Neither one of them realized that the gift was destined to become a spiritual cornerstone, not just for the Chinese but for all humankind. Neither one realized that one of the most significant events in human history had just taken place. This typical day at the Hangu Pass ... turned out to be not so typical after all.

The Origin of the Tao

This story of Lao Tzu at the pass is both memorable and useful for clearing up a number of points about the Tao and Taoism. Perhaps the most common misconception encountered by Westerners is that Lao Tzu himself was the founder of Taoism—which he was not. By the time Lao Tzu walked the Earth 2,500 years ago, the concept of the Tao had already been an integral part of Chinese culture for thousands of years. As the story puts it, Lao Tzu was looking to get away, not found a movement; by writing the Tao Te Ching, he was simply honoring a request to pass on the learning and knowledge of those who had preceded him.

The Tao Te Ching itself contains references to "ancient masters" or "masters of antiquity," terms referring not to Lao Tzu's contemporaries, as we may at first assume, but rather to people who were as ancient to him as he is to us. Two such ancient masters were Huang Ti (Pinyin *Huangdi*) and Fu Hsi (Pinyin *Fuxi;* pronounced *Fu Shi*). They were among the earliest rulers of China who lived more than 4,700 years ago—at least 2,200 years before Lao Tzu. Huang Ti has always been closely associated with the early form of Taoism, and Fu Hsi was the originator of the yin-and-yang concept.

Furthermore, it is interesting to note that Lao Tzu did not intend to write an expression of original ideas. Instead, he summarized existing ideas and teachings to create an overview of prevailing concepts. We know from Chinese oral tradition that one of Lao Tzu's primary sources was the library of King Wu. Although this library had an impressive collection, it still did not possess every notable book known to the ancients at that time—after all, King Wu was not the emperor of China, but only one of many lords vying for that title. Therefore, Lao Tzu's overview was almost comprehensive, but not quite.

In time, other sages of ancient China understood what Lao Tzu was trying to accomplish, and over the next seven centuries they added to his work wherever they noticed gaps. This gave rise to the historically verifiable fact that multiple early versions of the Tao Te Ching existed. Each was a work in progress as the sages who came after Lao Tzu changed a few words and shifted the order of the chapters. This process continued until about 1,800 years ago, when noted scholar Wang Bi consolidated the myriad editing changes and finalized the compilation.

These multiple versions of the Tao Te Ching have led some modern-day scholars to theorize that perhaps "Lao Tzu" is a composite of multiple individuals and never existed as a single historical figure.

People may assume that the question of Lao Tzu's historical existence must be as important to Taoists as Jesus' historical existence is to Christians, but it is not. Students of the Tao follow principles rather than particular individuals. The message is the central thing; the messenger is merely the conduit. Thus, the issue of historicity does not in the least diminish the importance of the Tao Te Ching or the power of its teachings.

Lao Tzu had created something so accessible that subsequent philosophers built on it and developed what we now know as Philosophical

Taoism, characterized by its secular observation of the natural laws governing existence. At the same time, spiritual seekers built on it in a different way to create Religious Taoism, marked by doctrines, rituals, and a pantheon of deities. Lao Tzu can be properly credited as the one who started these two parallel threads that became mainstays of Chinese culture. At the same time, the original form of Taoism that inspired him should also be recognized as the true source.

The incredibly ancient history of the Tao means that we can use the Tao Te Ching as a gateway to the distant past. When we study and practice it, we are not only bringing these words to life in our present circumstances, we are also leveraging Lao Tzu's words from 2,500 years ago to vault further back in time. Through Lao Tzu, we are extending our reach all the way to antiquity and connecting with the essence of the Chinese spirit since time immemorial.

Interfaith Approach

One reason Taoism has such durability is, paradoxically, because of its flexible and inclusive nature. Upon hearing it for the first time, many people assume the word *Tao* to be a specialized term specific to Taoism. In Chinese culture, however, it has always been a generic term applicable to every aspect of life, including *every conceivable religion,* because every belief system has its own particular way. The ancient Chinese sages who originated the term were perhaps the first practitioners of the interfaith approach to spirituality. Following their lead, Chinese people throughout history have applied the term to every school of thought and every discipline, including martial arts.

The original conception of Tao was simply the observation that reality has a certain way about it. This "way" encompasses all of existence: life, the universe, and everything. A Christian may call it God's will; an atheist may call it the laws of nature. These are labels pointing to the same thing, and Tao is simply the most generalized label imaginable, applicable to both perspectives.

Because of the Tao's inclusive nature, when Buddhism entered China 1,800 years ago, it found easy acceptance despite its differences from Taoism. A sense of optimism and humor runs throughout the ancient Tao, aptly expressed as "carefree wandering." Buddhism, on the other hand, saw life as *ku hai*, the bitter ocean, and focused on suffering. Despite this, Chinese people regarded Buddhist teachings as simply another way to express the Tao, thus setting the stage for Religious Taoism and Buddhism to interact and influence one another. By the time the Indian monk Bodhidharma visited China several hundred years later, it was only natural that a fusion of Indian and Chinese thought would give rise to Zen Buddhism.

This inclusive and unifying aspect of the Tao is something that is still not well understood in the West, and can lead to confusion about the similarities and differences between Taoism and Buddhism. It can also lead to an idea expressed by some Western authors that Taoism is opposed to another prominent Chinese tradition, Confucianism, which—contrasted to Taoism—is a philosophical framework on the interrelated functions of the individual and society, almost entirely devoid of spiritual commentary. While this confrontational model may be easy to grasp from a perspective that sees life in terms of battling forces, it is definitely not how the ancient sages viewed the Tao. To them, the Tao was a paradigm that encompassed everything. Although Religious Taoism did compete against Confucianism for the official designation as the philosophical basis of the empire, Chinese people throughout the centuries have been very comfortable subscribing to both camps, seeing them as complementary to one another, each useful in its own way.

In the West, the Tao has veered away from its generic roots and taken on an aura of exotic mystique. Those of us who cling to this misconception may be surprised to encounter Asians who casually speak of the Tao of Jesus or the Tao of science. On the other hand, if we connect with the original meaning, we will see that the Tao is truly for everyone, regardless of religious orientation—or lack thereof.

Furthermore, understanding the Tao helps remove us from a frame of mind that demands strict dualistic, either-or categories. To a mind that works in such dualisms, the question "Do you believe in God?" may be perfectly sensible. Yet, from the all-encompassing Taoist point of view, asking "Do you believe in the Tao?" makes as much sense as "Do you believe in your height?" Everyone has a certain height; this is something not subject to belief or disbelief. Similarly, everyone has a particular way—a uniquely individual outlook on life—and there is nothing we can do to affirm or deny it. Therefore, no one has to abandon or compromise his or her faith in order to "believe" in the Tao. Your Tao has always been and will always be a part of you.

In this all-inclusive sense, every one of us is already on a path of some sort, so we are all travelers on the Tao. Those of us who become aware of this and actively seek further understanding by studying the ancient Chinese sages are part of a more specialized group. We are not necessarily Taoists in the religious sense, but we cultivate the Tao in our lives, so the term *Tao cultivator* can be an appropriate designation. Membership in this group requires nothing more than an active interest in the Tao; by picking up this book you have already made yourself part of this time-honored tradition.

One characteristic of Tao cultivators is the understanding that the Tao does not have to be personified. It is the Ultimate Principle, not a supernatural being with human traits. Therefore, using a flame—a manifestation of energy—to represent it is better than using a painting or a sculpture of some human likeness. This is why the Mu Light is on the cover of this book. *Mu* is a reference to the nurturing nature of the Tao; *Light* represents divinity. The inscription behind the flame reads *wu ji*, meaning "without boundaries" and referring to the infinity of existence. When lit, the Mu Light casts its shadows through the inscription, symbolizing the way reality reflects the patterns of the Great Tao.

Ultimate Purpose

The ultimate purpose of the Tao Te Ching is to provide us with wisdom and insights that we can apply to life. If we cannot do that, then it doesn't matter how well we understand the passages. The true Tao must be lived.

At the cosmic level, the Tao of the macrocosm is represented by the laws of physics. They describe the universe and its manifestations, such as light, electricity, gravity, and so on. These things exist and have real effects no matter what we think of them. The gravity of the sun exerts its pull on the planets whether we "believe" in it or not.

At the personal level, the Tao of the microcosm is no less descriptive and useful. Its principles describe the human sphere and its manifestations, such as love, hate, peace, violence, and so on. These principles are just as real as the laws of physics; they function just as predictably and inexorably regardless of our opinions.

Lao Tzu's purpose is to illustrate these principles. If we can understand interpersonal forces among people as clearly as we understand interplanetary forces among heavenly bodies, then we, too, can glide through life as effortlessly and precisely as spacecraft flying through the solar system. The ultimate worth of any translation depends on how well it achieves Lao Tzu's purpose.

In the West, study of the Tao has led to mixed results. Generally speaking, people understand the all-encompassing, freewheeling nature of the Tao quite well, but they do not connect as easily with Lao Tzu's guidelines about life that require sustained effort. The result is that many who study the Tao end up with a form of relativism—thinking that because the Tao includes everything, whatever they do is already part of the Tao. Thus the Tao becomes the justification for any actions, positive or negative, as well as the all-purpose excuse for any results, or the lack thereof. This was never the original intent of the Tao Te Ching.

The truth is that the Tao isn't just about freedom and personal liberty; it is also about discipline and diligence. While everything in existence is indeed the Tao, our path through existence is also the Tao. This may seem like a paradox, but it really isn't. We can see it clearly by following the thought process of the sages. Think of existence as a forest. When we are in the forest, we have the ability to go forth in any direction. The forest doesn't care which path we take. It is the nature of the forest to offer all directions and all possibilities. This is *the way of the forest*—in other words, *the Tao of existence*.

We can wander in the forest aimlessly for as long as we wish, but at a certain point some of us will be ready to choose a destination and go there. This destination may represent enlightenment, salvation, true happiness, or other spiritual goals. Let us think of the destination as a mountain that we, walking in the forest, can glimpse through the tree branches from time to time.

There are paths in the forest that will take us to the mountain. These paths are easy to traverse and are marked by those who went before us. Inexperienced travelers may not be able to recognize the markings, but the Tao Te Ching is a map that can help us. When we follow the map, we move in a particular direction with a particular purpose. The progress we make is *our way through the forest*—in other words, *our Tao through existence*.

Thus, the Tao indeed encompasses all, just as we have the freedom to pick any direction in the forest and start walking. At the same time, our Tao must also be highly specific, just as we must choose one path out of many in the forest with care and foresight, if we wish to get somewhere and achieve our purpose in life, whatever that purpose may be. Therefore, this book's most important mission is to express the Tao *completely* as much as words can, conveying not only the encompassing aspect of the Tao but also its specific nature. To miss either attribute would be to fail the mission.

Let us keep the forest and the mountain in mind as we digest each chapter. Where are you in life? Where are you going? These are some of the most important questions we can ask ourselves. The more we understand what Lao Tzu says, the more clearly we will be able to see the markings that direct us to the proven path. We will then be able to formulate better answers and take steps in the direction that will lead us to our goal.

What will happen when we reach the summit? We will look around and take in the magnificent, panoramic view. From the vantage point at the top, we will be able to see other mountains in the hazy distance. We may rest for a bit; we may spend a moment in celebration. Then, we will start out for the next destination, savoring every breath of fresh air and every sight of natural beauty.

As Lao Tzu remarks in chapter 64, the journey of a thousand miles begins beneath your feet. As you embark on this journey, I wish you happy trails.

A Note on the Translation

Test of Time

In 2004, the College Board surveyed high schools to gauge interest in Advanced Placement courses in Chinese. The College Board expected a few hundred schools to express interest. What they found was substantially more: 2,400, or about ten times the level of interest they expected.

As East and West continue to draw together, the language barrier will diminish. The more this process continues, the more people will be able to assess Tao Te Ching translations for themselves, and demand ever higher levels of quality and fidelity to the original Chinese. I believe this is inevitable, and I want this book to be the one that withstands the test of time. No matter how rigorous the standard, this translation you hold in your hands will meet and surpass it.

My Approach

When I began translating the Tao Te Ching, I quickly realized that I needed a plan to avoid potential pitfalls and ensure as much accuracy and authenticity as possible. None of the commercially available translations withstood scrutiny. If I wished to produce a different result, I should try an approach not previously taken. Over time, I settled on the following four methods:

1. Start from scratch and create an entirely original work. I could not use existing translations as references because they were not sufficiently accurate. Any similarity between this translation and others would be purely coincidental.

2. Overcome the English-Chinese language barrier by bringing native
   fluency of both languages to the project. This alone would address
   many issues, since nearly all Tao Te Ching translators possess unbalanced levels of language proficiency.
3. Reference Chinese commentaries. The unbroken tradition of Tao Te
   Ching teachings began two thousand years ago and has continued to the present time. Although no living person can claim to
   possess native fluency in ancient Chinese, the commentaries give
   us the next best thing. They are like a window to the past.
4. Consult the ultimate experts on the Tao. I was fortunate in having
   access to Taoist masters from the I-Kuan Tao lineage. Their
   knowledge of the Tao comes from lifelong study as well as practical application. I drew upon their knowledge to make my presentation of the Tao as authentic as possible; I also followed their
   example in putting the Tao to the test, to verify its truth through
   actual usage.

As I followed this plan, I continued to compare my work in progress with
existing translations and noticed an additional problem common to them
all: a tendency to blur the line between translation and interpretation.
A literal translation (also known as formal equivalence) is the nearest
linguistic equivalent between the source and target language, while an
interpretation (also known as dynamic equivalence) consists of amplifica-
tions and clarifications, and so contains a lot more of the translator's personal opinions. Existing translations tended to present interpretations as
translations.

Much of this was due to format. Most editions included few or no
annotations or explanations, so the translator perhaps felt compelled to
explain the original within the translation itself. This process necessarily
engaged the translator's understanding. Thus, what might have started
out as a literal translation got twisted more and more into an expression of
the translator's thoughts.

This is why the volume you now hold in your hands is so revolutionary.
Its format allows for an extremely faithful rendition of the original that

adds nothing and subtracts nothing, while providing explanations on the opposite page, clearly marked as such. With this format, I can preserve the original and still clarify its meaning, and you will never have to wonder whether some particular words come from Lao Tzu or from me. The difference between the two will be unmistakable, so you can judge the interpretation for yourself.

Pronunciation and Romanization

One of the first specific challenges I had to address in creating a new translation concerned how to spell words in English to reflect their pronunciation in Chinese. For example, although *Tao* is traditionally spelled with the letter *t*, it is meant to be pronounced with the *d* sound, like *Dow* in Dow Jones. Similarly, *Tao Te Ching* should be pronounced like *Dao De Jing*. There are other terms in the study of the Tao that do not sound like the way they look. This is the result of romanization—the transliteration of Chinese characters using English letters—and it can be confusing.

The first Chinese romanization system was Wade-Giles, created about a hundred years ago. The earliest Western scholars who studied Chinese had neither prior work to guide them nor significant assistance from native speakers. Their system required specialized knowledge to use correctly, but that knowledge remained trapped in academic obscurity and never made it out to the mainstream. Confusion about this system is so pervasive that, even today, many who claim expertise about the Tao continue to mispronounce or misspell Chinese words. Even the Chinese themselves get confused, despite knowing how their own language sounds. They have, in effect, adopted Western mistakes as their own.

In an attempt to address this issue, Chinese scholars have created a new standard to replace Wade-Giles: the Pinyin system. This new standard resolves the problems highlighted above but introduces new ones. For instance, Pinyin's use of the letters *x*, *c*, and *q* can be misleading to most English speakers. It is also likely that problems will worsen as people liberally mix the two systems without really understanding either one.

In this book, I deal with this confusing situation by using the following three guidelines:

1. If a term romanized with Wade-Giles is already well known, it will remain unchanged, to conform with the common, established usage.
2. If a term is not well known, it will be romanized with the Pinyin system to conform to the new standard established by mainland China for the future.
3. Wherever either system produces confusing results, pronunciation assistance will be provided parenthetically.

Holistic Understanding

Another challenge I faced in creating the most accurate translation possible has to do with the Chinese language itself, which has evolved a lot over the centuries. Many ancient characters are no longer in modern usage, and some characters have taken on new meanings. The syntax has also changed so that native speakers of modern Chinese can find the ancient form quite baffling. All of this can lead to misunderstanding. The best way to avoid this misunderstanding is to approach the Tao Te Ching as a whole and use the entire book to help us understand individual chapters.

One example to illustrate this comes from line 3 of chapter 1. It starts with the characters *wu ming*, which mean "not having" and "name" respectively. Together, they can be translated as "nameless." Thus, the entire line means "The nameless is the origin of Heaven and Earth." This is the classical interpretation. Another school of thought is that there should be a pause after *wu*, thus making it a noun instead of an adjective. The translation then becomes "The state of nonexistence is the name for the origin of Heaven and Earth" or "Nonexistence is named the origin of Heaven and Earth." Scholars who support this new interpretation feel that it makes more sense.

The concept of punctuation marks is unknown in ancient Chinese, so there may or may not be a pause after *wu*. If we cannot tell one way or the other, does that mean both interpretations are equally valid? Not necessarily. We can distinguish between the two by checking other chapters of the Tao Te Ching. If *wu ming* is clearly used to say "nameless" in other chapters, then the classical interpretation is more likely to be correct. On the other hand, if other chapters show *ming* being used in the same way as the new interpretation, then that would give credence to the new interpretation.

Chapters 32, 37, and 41 all feature the use of *wu ming*. In these chapters, *wu ming* can only be translated as "nameless," due to unambiguous context. This is a powerful endorsement of the classical interpretation. Chapter 14 demonstrates that when Lao Tzu uses *ming* in the way suggested by the new interpretation, he adds the character *yue* to remove the ambiguity. Because the *yue* character cannot be found anywhere in chapter 1, this becomes evidence against the new interpretation.

This example illustrates how tricky it can be for us to approach the Tao Te Ching. It also underlines the importance of reading the entire book as an integrated whole, so we can see the common threads from various chapters and how they reinforce one another. This approach is the way to go if we wish to understand Lao Tzu's teachings as clearly as possible.

The Language Barrier

Even with these strategies in place, however, I still had to deal with the fundamental barrier between Chinese and English. Chinese comes from linguistic roots that are entirely different from those of European languages, and rendering an understandable yet accurate translation can be difficult to achieve. Specifically, I wanted to pay special attention to vocabularly and word choice to avoid the errors common to many other translations of the Tao Te Ching.

Few translators possess native command of both languages, and the result is the greatly varying quality of translations available today. Inaccurate translations do a disservice to the reader because they may distort the original meaning or even obscure it completely. We may end up with something that bears little resemblance to the original, genuine wisdom—and we may not be aware of what we are missing. Chapter 46 is an example of this. It starts with the image of fast horses, formerly used by the army for scouting missions, being retired to till the fields. This is the ancient Chinese equivalent of beating swords into plowshares, as well as a deft depiction of peace and harmony. Lao Tzu then contrasts it with the description of a pregnant mare being forced to give birth in the middle of the battlefield—a singularly powerful image that evokes the misery and horrors of war.

What happens when this chapter goes through the translation process? In one popular version, all references to horses have disappeared, replaced by factories, trucks, tractors, warheads, and cities. None of these things can be found in the original text, and—obviously—none of them existed in ancient China. This creative license is clearly an interpretation, not a translation. Even more important, it denies the reader the beauty and power of the original vision.

Sometimes translators may guess at the meaning of a character without consulting a dictionary. For instance, some have rendered the first line of the Tao Te Ching as "the path that can be trodden," guessing that dao, the character for the Tao or the path, should mean "to walk" when used as a verb. Some scholars also assert that this is the original meaning, which differs from modern usage. However, there is no compelling evidence to support this assertion, and it contradicts virtually all Chinese commentaries on chapter 1.

When used as a verb, dao can only mean "to speak, to talk, to discuss." Walking simply isn't one of the definitions. Therefore, to translate the first line as "the path that can be trodden" is like saying "I am waying" in English when you really mean "I am walking." This is not a valid usage because "way" doesn't have that meaning. It is the same with dao.

Another example of distortion is the "uncarved block," a concept that everyone studying the Tao will come across sooner or later. It is a reference to pu, the Taoist principle of simplicity. The uncarved block refers to things in their original, primal state, filled with the inherent power of potential and possibilities, before that power is lost to human contrivance as the block is carved into a specific form.

In modern Chinese, *pu* means "plain." In ancient Chinese, it can also mean "plain wood." Either way, the meaning of *pu* does not include a block of any sort. Thus, "uncarved block" is actually a mistranslation. Plain wood represents the original state of simplicity far better than the uncarved block. A plain piece of wood may be found in nature, completely untouched by human hands. The uncarved block, on the other hand, has already been worked on—someone had to cut a plain piece of wood in order to get a block out of it. Therefore, "uncarved block" is more than just a mistranslation. It is also an obstruction to those who seek the authentic teaching.

Translation Techniques

Ultimately, my translation was an iterative process in which I took each semantic unit (a character, a word, or an expression) from the original text and searched for the best approximation in English. This search yielded results that fell into one of three possible categories.

The first category consists of words that have been formally accepted into the English language and show up in mainstream dictionaries. They should be used in a translation whenever possible for maximum accuracy. *Tao, chi, yin,* and *yang* are good examples. Not many words enjoy this level of acceptance, so this category remains sparse. Prior to *Tao* becoming an English word, it was acceptable to translate *dao* as "the Way." Now that Tao is part of our language, "the Way" can no longer be considered the optimal translation.

The second category consists of expressions that have a direct English equivalent. For instance, *tian di* means "Heaven and Earth," an expression that already exists in English, so *tian di* can be translated literally. Another example is *tian xia* (pronounced *shia*), which literally means "below heaven" or "under the sky." It can be translated as it is, except when the usage clearly means "the world."

The character *te* corresponds with the word *virtue* in a serendipitous way. Virtue means not only a human goodness (compassion, patience, generosity, etc.) but also an inherent power in all things. For instance, when we say "by virtue of being there, he witnessed the event" we are not saying "being there" is a positive human trait. We are saying that "being there" has an inherent power that enables what follows. *Te* has the same dual meaning, so it should therefore be mapped to "virtue" whenever possible. Some translators use "integrity," which loses the value of this correspondence.

The nearest equivalent to the character *ching* (pronounced *jing*) is "tome" or "classic." The widely used convention is "book," which has a different feel but is still acceptable. Therefore, a reasonable translation for Tao Te Ching is "Book of the Tao and Virtue." This is more accurate than "Book of the Way and Its Virtue" or "Book of the Tao and Its Power."

The third category consists of expressions that have no direct English equivalents and must be translated by meaning. For instance, *wu wei*, although well known to students of the Tao, has not yet made it into the English language. It cannot be left as it is in the translation, nor should it be translated into a misleading term such as "nonaction" or "without doing." The closest linguistic equivalent to *wu wei* is "detached action," or "acting without attachment."

Another prominent example in this category is *wan wu*, which literally means "ten thousand things." At the present time, "ten thousand things" exists in English as Taoist jargon; it is not part of the popular vernacular. Therefore, it should not be translated literally. The nearest linguistic equivalent to *wan wu* is "myriad things" or "all things."

Similarly, *shen ren* means "divine person"—someone so wise that his or her wisdom approaches the Divine. Several past attempts to translate this have yielded poor results. For instance, "holy man" and "saint" both carry religious connotations not found in the original. Another attempt, "evolved individual," carries the context of spiritual evolution, which is really a pet notion injected by the translator. The term "sage" is much closer to the original. (Other examples in this category, such as *chien li* and *bai xing*, can best be explained fully on the www.taoism.net website. The site offers a wealth of material specifically designed to complement this book. Please see Suggestions for Further Reading for additional details.)

A final piece of my translation work had to do with the use of punctuation. Although the concept of punctuation marks did not exist in ancient Chinese, the language did have its own specific ways of denoting various effects of speech. For example, a larger than usual gap between characters meant a slight pause, equivalent to a comma. Special characters at the end of a sentence served the same functions as the period, question mark, and exclamation point. These special characters are no longer used in modern Chinese, which has adopted a set of punctuation marks similar to punctuation used in English. In my translation, however, I wanted to approximate the open, porous feel of ancient Chinese—the native tongue of the Tao Te Ching—so I chose to omit periods and most other punctuation except where necessary for clarity.

The net effect of all these techniques is a translation that tunes in to the Tao Te Ching with maximum fidelity and minimum static. I understand that not everyone places as much importance on this as I do; at the same time, my opinion is that a translation for a sacred text should be a mirror that reflects the original as perfectly as possible. Warped mirrors may be amusing for the funhouse, but they are not so great for daily use, which is the ultimate goal of the Tao Te Ching—to be both an inspiration and a practical guide to your path through this life.

Tao Te Ching

1 The first line of the Tao Te Ching can be one of the most confusing. Some have interpreted it to mean that we must never speak of the Tao, or that if we try to explain it, then we must have no true understanding of it.

What it actually means is that we can never understand the Tao through the intellect alone. We must feel it. Talking about it can be useful but will never replace the actual experience of living it.

2 Not only is the Tao beyond the power of spoken words to describe, but it is also beyond the power of written words to define. That which can be defined is limited by the definition, and the Tao transcends all limitations.

3 Before the universe came into being, concepts and things did not exist, and no human consciousness was present to perceive and name them. Therefore, the Tao that initiated Creation was the ultimate nameless enigma.

4 Once the universe came into being, the stage was set for the physical manifestation of everything, including human beings. These humans eventually attained sufficient awareness to observe all things and name them.

5 Self-serving desires tend to limit us to a superficial level. If we think of other people and not just focus on ourselves, we will find it much easier to connect with the underlying reality. This applies to every aspect of life. It is one of the most powerful teachings of the Tao.

6 The two refer to manifestations (outer appearance) and essence (inner truth). They represent the material world and the spiritual realm respectively. Both emerge from the Tao, because the Tao encompasses all—not only spirituality but also the physical universe. The basic unity of the two is the mystery that we investigate in Tao cultivation.

1

The Tao that can be spoken is not the eternal Tao[1]
The name that can be named is not the eternal name[2]
The nameless is the origin of Heaven and Earth[3]
The named is the mother of myriad things[4]
Thus, constantly without desire, one observes its essence
Constantly with desire, one observes its manifestations[5]
These two emerge together but differ in name
The unity is said to be the mystery
Mystery of mysteries, the door to all wonders[6]

1 Tao sages have long recognized the relative nature of the world. Values have meaning only in comparison. For instance, a task can only be "easy" if we compare it to some other task that is more difficult. If there is nothing else to compare it with, the task cannot be rated in terms of difficulty.

2 Similarly, we can only say an object is "long" if we are comparing it to another similar object that is shorter. Each half of a duality cannot exist without the other. A descriptive concept creates its own opposite. This relative concept applies to everything, even good and evil.

What about absolute good and evil? Do they exist in the Tao? While we can certainly find absolutes in abstract theory, in the real world they rarely, if ever, exist. For instance, no metal is absolutely free of impurities. In fact, hardly anything in nature is absolutely pure. We can get close to 100 percent purity but never quite reach that absolute state.

It is the same with people. Absolute good and evil can exist as concepts, but we will never find them in human beings. We are all mixtures of varying proportions. None of us is any one thing.

2

When the world knows beauty as beauty, ugliness arises
When it knows good as good, evil arises
Thus being and nonbeing produce each other
Difficult and easy bring about each other[1]
Long and short reveal each other
High and low support each other
Music and voice harmonize each other
Front and back follow each other[2]
Therefore the sages:
Manage the work of detached actions
Conduct the teaching of no words
They work with myriad things but do not control
They create but do not possess
They act but do not presume
They succeed but do not dwell on success
It is because they do not dwell on success
That it never goes away

1 When we glorify achievers and set them aside for special treatment, people will compete aggressively and step over one another to achieve that glory. Similarly, when we place a high value on certain goods, there will be those who plot to take them by force or by trickery.

This determination of value can be rather arbitrary. For instance, what intrinsic goodness does gold have that makes it so much more valuable than other metals? What is so great about gold other than a particular numerical value that people determine and agree upon? In general, whenever we point to anything as desirable, a wave of disruption ripples through society. People begin to think of ways to get more of the desirable thing, often at the expense of others.

Because of this, a sagacious ruler refrains from setting aside certain individuals for glorification, or designating certain goods as extremely valuable and putting them on display. These are surefire ways of stimulating materialistic desire, which is a bottomless pit.

2 Although the sages empty people's hearts of desires and reduce their ambitions for fame, glory, or material wealth, they also pay particular attention to their basic needs. As rulers, the sages see to it that the people enjoy good health and do not go hungry. As teachers, the sages give people teachings that provide spiritual sustenance and promote spiritual health.

3 When people follow the way of the sages, the few who scheme and plot will find themselves unable to utilize their repertoire of clever ploys. The governance of the sages leaves no room for their contrived tactics, and everything falls into place peacefully and naturally.

3

Do not glorify the achievers
So the people will not squabble
Do not treasure goods that are hard to obtain
So the people will not become thieves
Do not show the desired things
So their hearts will not be confused[1]

Thus the governance of the sage:
Empties their hearts
Fills their bellies
Weakens their ambitions
Strengthens their bones[2]

Let the people have no cunning and no greed
So those who scheme will not dare to meddle[3]

Act without contrivance
And nothing will be beyond control

1 The emptiness of the Tao is not a vacuous state of nothingness, because its infinite depths conceal the seeds of Creation. There appears to be nothing in the Tao, and yet it contains everything. It is the "pregnant void," a field of unlimited potentialities.

One way to describe the Tao is to compare it with an empty container with infinite capacity. This container cannot be filled up, and the water that flows out of it can never be used up. It continues to function indefinitely.

2 The Tao is eternal. It outlasts everything. After millions of years, even the tallest, sharpest mountain peaks will be reduced to gentle rolling hills. After billions of years, even the brightest stars will burn out and shine no more.

Given enough time, all problems great and small will be resolved one way or another, like the unraveling of even the tightest knots. Given enough time, even the proudest achievements of humankind will be reduced to dust.

3 The indistinct nature of the Tao refers to the fact that we cannot perceive it directly. We can only observe its effects on the world, just as we can see the effects of gravity (objects falling) but never gravity itself.

4 We do not know how the Tao came to be, or whether it came from anywhere at all. Does the concept of "place" have meaning without the Tao? Does the ultimate source have a source? We cannot say. We cannot pretend to have all the answers.

5 "Emperor" in this line refers to *Yu Di*, the Jade Emperor. He is the ruler of the universe and the supreme deity in ancient Chinese mythology. Lao Tzu is saying that the image of the Tao precedes even such a being, because any principles that govern the divine must, by definition, be part of the Tao. Therefore, the Tao has to be *already present* before anything like a supreme deity can manifest existence.

4

The Tao is empty
When utilized, it is not filled up[1]
So deep! It seems to be the source of all things

It blunts the sharpness
Unravels the knots
Dims the glare
Mixes the dusts[2]

So indistinct! It seems to exist[3]
I do not know whose offspring it is[4]
Its image is the predecessor of the Emperor[5]

1 The original Chinese characters *bu ren* are often mistranslated as "ruthless" or "without compassion." This produces statements at odds with reality, because real-life sages are compassionate individuals—hardly ruthless.

The true meaning of *bu ren* is that the Tao does not play favorites. The rain waters weeds and orchids equally; the sun shines on everyone with the same brightness and warmth despite variations in individual merits. The sage, in emulating the Tao, also regards everyone in the same egalitarian light—none higher and none lower.

2 Straw dogs are literally small dog figurines made from straw. They were used in ancient times for rituals, and then discarded after use. It is a striking metaphor when we consider how we are similar to the straw dogs. We are here to go through the ritual called life; when the ritual is done there is no further use for the physical body, so it is discarded.

3 "Too many words" here means too much bureaucracy, or too many rules and regulations.

4 I have translated the last character, *zhong*, as "quiet." This can be confusing even to native Chinese speakers. According to the dictionary, it means "middle" or "center." Thus, one may assume the last line has to do with centering oneself or holding on to the principle of moderation. This is probably not correct, because the previous line is not about the danger of extremes.

The real meaning of *zhong*, in ancient times and in this particular context, is silence. When we see how the maddening "noise" of complex bureaucracy and too many laws hasten failure, we would naturally want to reach for its opposite—the quietness of simplicity.

5 □

Heaven and Earth are impartial[1]
And regard myriad things as straw dogs
The sages are impartial
And regard people as straw dogs[2]

The space between Heaven and Earth
Is it not like a bellows?
Empty, and yet never exhausted
It moves, and produces more

Too many words hasten failure[3]
Cannot compare to keeping quiet[4]

1 The spirit of the valley is a powerful symbol for yin, the universal female principle. It is eternal; it has always existed and will always exist. This principle has many names. We can call it the sacred feminine, or the Mystic Female.

2 The Mystic Female is the ultimate source of all living things. The ancient Chinese noted that women were responsible for the miracle of life, and therefore had to possess a measure of divine power. They respected this power and regarded it as the basis of existence (the root of Heaven and Earth).

3 The essence of life itself is a continuous flow. We may take it for granted and not pay attention to it, but it is always there. Because life begets life, its power extends indefinitely into the future. It does not matter how much we utilize; we can never use it up.

As Tao cultivators, we are in tune with this essence. We recognize the goddess in every woman and celebrate the sacred power of the feminine. Let us be mindful of the truth that we all come from the Mystic Female, without which none of us can exist.

6 □

The valley spirit, undying
Is called the Mystic Female[1]

The gateway of the Mystic Female
Is called the root of Heaven and Earth[2]

It flows continuously, barely perceptible
When utilized, it is never exhausted[3]

1 Heaven and Earth perform their functions without selfish desires. When we emulate this aspect of nature, we think of others first and ourselves last. By letting go of self-centered thoughts, we can feel the way our inner nature mirrors the greater Tao. When we let this natural mirroring process take place without interference, we become like Heaven and Earth—existing to be of service to others.

2 A genuine, selfless desire to be helpful inspires people and wins their respect. Although sages have no wish to draw attention, people single them out and look to them for leadership. Although the sages place themselves last out of humility, the people push them to the forefront, into positions of responsibility.

Long after the sages have passed on, memories of them endure. People continue to remember with reverence their words and actions. Just like Heaven and Earth, the legacy of the sages lasts forever.

3 To be "outside of oneself" in this context means to be unconcerned with one's well-being, to disregard one's body, or to sacrifice oneself. This can be seen as another Tao paradox: we can advance our own "selfish" agenda by being totally selfless.

Lao Tzu was a good example of this. He was content to be a humble, unknown philosopher. He never sought fame and recognition; he never claimed to be divine in any way. And yet here we are reading his words, which have survived the last twenty-five centuries and will continue on long after we are gone.

Make it a point to put this teaching into practice, and see what happens. Spend an entire day living this selfless mindset. You'll discover the world responding to you in wonderful and even miraculous ways.

7 □

Heaven and Earth are everlasting
The reason Heaven and Earth can last forever
Is that they do not exist for themselves
Thus they can last forever[1]

Therefore the sages:
Place themselves last but end up in front[2]
Are outside of themselves and yet survive
Is it not all due to their selflessness?
That is how they can achieve their own goals[3]

1 Water is the most fitting metaphor for the Tao. Water always flows to the lowest place, not because it is forced to do so, but because it follows its own nature. We also place ourselves lower, not because we contrive to do so, but because it is our nature to be humble.

2 A deep pool of water is much more than its surface. Likewise, there is more to a Tao cultivator than meets the eye. The more people get to know us, the more they will discover.

3 Water provides its benefits and moves on, without waiting for any benefits in return. We benefit others in the same way. When we provide assistance, we do so with no strings attached.

4 Water reflects its surroundings and does not hide or change anything in its reflection. We conduct ourselves with this same sense of integrity and accuracy. People come to trust us, because they realize we will give them the truth when no one else will.

5 Water administers to everything equally. It slakes the thirst of the kind person just as it does the unkind person. Thus, we also do not pick and choose the recipients of the benefits we provide.

6 Water is versatile. It conforms to the shape of any container. Following this, we also cultivate flexibility and adaptability. Because the world is continually changing, we make constant adjustments to handle new challenges.

7 Whether it takes the form of rain or snow, water follows the timing of natural events. We are the same way. We live each day following its natural flow, and take appropriate actions at the appropriate times.

8 Water gives itself to everything without protest. Like water, we do not engage in petty squabbles, because our only wish is to be of service.

The highest goodness resembles water
Water greatly benefits myriad things without contention
It stays in places that people dislike
Therefore it is similar to the Tao[1]

Dwelling at the right place
Heart with great depth[2]
Giving with great kindness[3]
Words with great integrity[4]
Governing with great administration[5]
Handling with great capability[6]
Moving with great timing[7]

Because it does not contend
It is therefore beyond reproach[8]

1 Moderation and restraint are crucial to life. The sages note that an overflowing cup isn't necessarily a good thing, because the area around the cup gets wet and messy very quickly. It is better to stop short of fullness. Similarly, if you pound a blade repeatedly and sharpen it too much, it will break easily and won't last very long.

In general, doing anything to excess is a bad idea. The smarter way is to do just enough and nothing extra. When in doubt, stop just short of the point that you think is the optimum.

2 A room that is full of treasures is like an overflowing cup. It becomes the target of thieves and robbers and cannot be safeguarded forever. Arrogance as the result of great wealth or high position is like a blade that has been sharpened too much. It is an invitation to disaster.

3 To withdraw oneself does not mean to retreat from society and become a hermit. It means there is no need to brag about your achievements, take on pompous airs, or put on showy displays. Once you have achieved success and fame, it is best to step gracefully, quietly aside.

9 □

Holding a cup and overfilling it
Cannot be as good as stopping short
Pounding a blade and sharpening it
Cannot be kept for long[1]

Gold and jade fill up the room
No one is able to protect them
Wealth and position bring arrogance
And leave disasters upon oneself[2]

When achievement is completed, fame is attained
Withdraw oneself[3]
This is the Tao of Heaven

1 "Straying" refers to deviating from centered oneness, caused by the distractions of the material. Some translations render it as "separation" or "division," thus obscuring the original meaning and making these lines more difficult to understand.

2 The energy to be concentrated is chi—the breath or energy that courses through all living things. This is a clear instruction on using breathing techniques to achieve a deep level of relaxation, where the body is as soft and pliant as that of an infant.

3 These lines may seem to be directed at kings and emperors, but they actually address the individual as well. Think of the kingdom as a metaphor for your workplace, family, social circle, sports team, and even your immediate surroundings, and the practical utility of this section becomes clear.

4 The feminine principle refers to the yin principle of serenity and quietude. The opening and closing of the gate refers to the mind in motion and at rest. Together, these two lines describe a mental state that remains tranquil even when thought processes are active—a state that is simultaneously peaceful and dynamic.

5 Sages emulate the Mystic Virtue in their interactions with other people. They nurture, encourage, teach, and mentor those around them without the need to possess, gloat, or dominate.

10

In holding the soul and embracing oneness
Can one be steadfast, without straying?[1]
In concentrating the energy and reaching relaxation
Can one be like an infant?[2]
In cleaning away the worldly view
Can one be without imperfections?
In loving the people and ruling the nation
Can one be without manipulation?[3]
In the heavenly gate's opening and closing
Can one hold to the feminine principle?[4]
In understanding clearly all directions
Can one be without intellectuality?

Bearing it, rearing it
Bearing without possession
Achieving without arrogance
Raising without domination
This is called the Mystic Virtue[5]

1 We tend to associate substance with usefulness, and dismiss the lack of substance as useless. Lao Tzu goes against this thinking and points out the very opposite. The hole in the hub of the wheel allows the axle to go through. Therefore, it is the emptiness there, not the substance, that gives the wheel its crucial functionality as part of a carriage. There is more to emptiness than meets the eye.

2 The same is true for containers. While we cannot dispute that the substance of the container is necessary, we also must admit that it is the empty space in the container that allows it to contain. Without that emptiness, the container would not be functional at all.

3 We can think of rooms as containers of people. As such, they also require both substance and emptiness in order to function. The walls of a room must accommodate emptiness, and we need at least one opening in one wall to access a room. We simply cannot do without emptiness.

We can also think of the Tao as the ultimate container, because everything is embedded in the Tao. It then follows automatically that it is the emptiness of the Tao that gives it power and functionality. How can it be that everything comes from the Tao? The emptiness makes it so.

11

Thirty spokes join in one hub
In its emptiness, there is the function of a vehicle[1]
Mix clay to create a container
In its emptiness, there is the function of a container[2]
Cut open doors and windows to create a room
In its emptiness, there is the function of a room

Therefore, that which exists is used to create benefit
That which is empty is used to create functionality[3]

1 The five colors, five sounds, and five flavors denote the vast array of sensory stimulations in the material world. Excessive indulgence in these stimulations leads to sensory overload, followed by fatigue, numbness, boredom, and apathy.

This is more true than ever in today's world, with its virtually endless entertainment options. To compensate for our dull and jaded senses, we turn the intensity of sensory stimuli way up. This gives us a temporary thrill, but soon it fades. We return to a dismal state of dissatisfaction, which drives us to seek even greater thrills.

2 I have translated the key character in this line, *shuang*, as "tasteless." This can cause confusion. In modern Chinese it means "refreshing," which is a positive feeling not at all congruent with blindness or deafness in the previous two lines.

This is a perfect example of where the ancient usage of the character is very different from the modern meaning. In this context, the true definition of *shuang* is a negative connotation. When combined with *ko*, the character for mouth, it means "loss of taste." This negative connotation has not completely disappeared from modern Chinese. For instance, *shuang yue* means "failing to show up for a date or an appointment."

3 Caring for the stomach means focusing on one's basic needs and living life with plainness. Caring for the eyes means acquiring even more sensory stimuli, more "eye candy." The former is the only sure cure for sensory overindulgence, and that is why the sages embrace it and discard the latter. They let go of the many temptations of the material world and reach for the simplicity of the Tao.

12 □

The five colors make one blind in the eyes
The five sounds make one deaf in the ears[1]
The five flavors make one tasteless in the mouth[2]

Racing and hunting make one wild in the heart
Goods that are difficult to acquire make one cause damage

Therefore the sages care for the stomach and not the eyes
That is why they discard the other and take this[3]

1 We may not wish to admit it, but most of us care very much what other people think. We fret over positive opinions as well as negative ones. It isn't just the prospect of being ridiculed that makes us anxious; we also feel anxiety over not receiving accolades that we feel we deserve. It cuts both ways.

2 "Self" refers to the ego, which we can see is at the heart of this issue. An inflated sense of self-importance causes us to become attached to the praise and approval of our peers. It also causes us to fear disapproval and rejection. This is why Lao Tzu sees it as the leading source of adversity and trouble—the greatest misfortune.

3 This is the recipe for managing the ego. Note that Lao Tzu does not advocate that we should be completely without ego, or that we should eliminate it. We need at least a moderate sense of self to function in society. Therefore, it's perfectly fine to value and love the ego—as long as we don't focus so much on ourselves that we neglect the world.

As Tao cultivators, we love and value the world. Our caution against the sensory stimuli of the material world does not make us distant or uncaring. We can be joyously involved with the world and yet totally unaffected by its temptations and distractions.

Favor and disgrace make one fearful
The greatest misfortune is the self
What does "favor and disgrace make one fearful" mean?
Favor is high; disgrace is low
Having it makes one fearful
Losing it makes one fearful
This is "favor and disgrace make one fearful"[1]

What does "the greatest misfortune is the self" mean?
The reason I have great misfortune
Is that I have the self
If I have no self
What misfortune do I have?[2]

So one who values the self as the world
Can be given the world
One who loves the self as the world[3]
Can be entrusted with the world

1 The Tao cannot be seen, heard, or touched because it is metaphysical in nature. Because it has no physical manifestations, it cannot be detected by any of our physical senses.

2 This means the characteristics of being colorless, noiseless, and formless must all be true. None of them stands alone. Together, they are central to the concept of the Tao.

3 Brightness and darkness only have meaning in something that can be seen. Because the Tao is invisible, it cannot be either bright or dark.

4 Although the Tao is immaterial, it gives all material things solid reality. Thus, the world we observe is the visible image of the imageless Tao. Similarly, all the things we can touch and hold are the tangible manifestations of the formless Tao.

5 The Tao is infinite in extent, not only in itself but also in its functions. It has no beginning and no end, so we cannot see its front or back. Concepts like "front" and "back" simply do not apply to something so utterly beyond limits.

6 This sounds like Lao Tzu is talking about us. We are indeed wielding the ancient Tao to manage modern life—and discovering that it works very well indeed. The sun rises today just as it did thousands of years ago. Similarly, the Tao holds true for us just as it held true for the ancients.

We can even say that the Tao works better now than it did long ago, because we don't have to reinvent the wheel. We can take advantage of the work that ancient sages have done to advance our understanding. We can see farther because we have the good fortune of standing on the shoulders of giants.

14 □

Look at it, it cannot be seen
It is called colorless
Listen to it, it cannot be heard
It is called noiseless
Reach for it, it cannot be held
It is called formless[1]
These three cannot be completely unraveled
So they are combined into one[2]

Above it, not bright
Below it, not dark[3]
Continuing endlessly, cannot be named
It returns back into nothingness
Thus it is called the form of the formless
The image of the imageless[4]
This is called enigmatic
Confront it, its front cannot be seen
Follow it, its back cannot be seen[5]

Wield the Tao of the ancients
To manage the existence of today[6]
One can know the ancient beginning
It is called the Tao Axiom

1 The concept of *emulation* is central to the Tao. The ancient masters recognized that they did not understand the Tao completely but that they could learn from it by emulating nature. We can learn from them in the same way.

2 The ancient masters were not given to frivolous or reckless acts. They handled responsibilities with serious regard; they resolved issues by carefully considering all sides, without jumping to conclusions.

3 The masters were careful, but not uptight. They went about their activities with a certain looseness, which took nothing away from their concern for others and for doing a good job. They could be relaxed without being lax, and thus achieve excellence effortlessly; they could be unattached without being uncaring, and thus focus on the process instead of the end result.

4 "Plain wood" is a reference to simplicity. By keeping everything simple, the ancient masters experienced the profound happiness of the uncomplicated present.

5 The ancient sages were known for their openness. They gladly considered new ideas without dismissing anything out of hand. They treated everyone, even difficult people, with infinite patience.

6 Being opaque means these masters never put themselves on display, despite their spiritual refinements. They had no interest in showing off their brilliance.

7 The image of muddy water becoming clear refers to the gradual revelation of a master's inner qualities. The masters had tremendous depth, so it would take time for people to really know them.

8 The serenity of a sage can be mistaken for passivity or apathy. It may be difficult for people to understand how anyone can embody tranquility and dynamism simultaneously.

9 The ancient masters were therefore never full of themselves. Like them, we can cultivate quietly, preserving a sense of calmness without drawing attention to ourselves or creating a disturbance.

15 ☐

The Tao masters of antiquity
Subtle wonders through mystery
Depths that cannot be discerned
Because one cannot discern them
Therefore one is forced to describe the appearance[1]

Hesitant, like crossing a wintry river
Cautious, like fearing four neighbors
Solemn, like a guest[2]
Loose, like ice about to melt[3]
Genuine, like plain wood[4]
Open, like a valley[5]
Opaque, like muddy water[6]

Who can be muddled yet desist
In stillness gradually become clear?[7]
Who can be serene yet persist
In motion gradually come alive?[8]

One who holds this Tao does not wish to be overfilled
Because one is not overfilled
Therefore one can preserve and not create anew[9]

1 Everything in nature exhibits a cyclic pattern: the changing seasons, the tides, the sun, the moon. All living things flourish and eventually return to their origin in the recurrent cycles of life. When we quiet the internal chatter and bear silent witness to the miraculous natural processes at work, we strengthen our connection with the empty, yet incredibly prolific, creativity of the Tao.

2 This is a precise description of what happens when we feel our essential oneness with nature. In that oneness, we find the gift of tranquility. We discover that nature is not merely all around us but also inside of us. Human nature is but a microcosm of the greater nature. The realization of this constant, unchanging principle brings us spiritual clarity. This clarity cannot be described in words and must be experienced firsthand.

3 Tao cultivators accept reality as it is, rather than as they wish it to be. The troubles we encounter in life and the pain associated with them are caused by the disparity between our expectations and the way things are. The more stubbornly we refuse to accept, the more we suffer.

4 To be sovereign is to possess authentic power—not power over other people, but power over oneself. It is the profound realization that we are ultimately responsible for creating our own reality. We have the ultimate authority over our own destiny. Our sacred task in life is to learn how to exercise this sovereign power wisely.

16 □

Attain the ultimate emptiness
Hold on to the truest tranquility
The myriad things are all active
I therefore watch their return[1]

Everything flourishes; each returns to its root
Returning to the root is called tranquility
Tranquility is called returning to one's nature
Returning to one's nature is called constancy
Knowing constancy is called clarity[2]

Not knowing constancy, one recklessly causes trouble
Knowing constancy is acceptance[3]
Acceptance is impartiality
Impartiality is sovereign
Sovereign is Heaven[4]
Heaven is Tao
Tao is eternal
The self is no more, without danger

1 The most skillful rulers work behind the scene. They know how to achieve their objectives quickly and quietly. They use a light touch and produce seamless results. They are so good at what they do that people are hardly aware of their existence.

Note: The original Chinese is not gender specific in referring to the ruler and does not assert that the ruler must be male. Most translators arbitrarily force the gender to be either male or female, which distorts the original meaning.

2 Below the level of ideal leadership, we have rulers who act in benevolent ways, so people love them; rulers who use intimidation, so people fear them; and rulers who are incompetent, so people despise them.

3 The ideal way is to govern in an unhurried manner, where rulers are bound by their words, and therefore never speak lightly. Such rulers tend to do more and talk less. This, in turn, means the affairs of the state are conducted in a nondisruptive way. The people, unaware of all the work that goes into governing, assume that they did it themselves.

Like several other passages from the Tao Te Ching, this chapter seems to be aimed at the ancient kings of China. How can such passages apply to us?

Do not think of ruling in the literal sense of leading a nation. Look at your own life and note all the circumstances where leadership plays a role. Most of us will, at some point, be called upon to play a leading role in social settings, community activities, or the workplace.

The Tao of leadership remains constant in any context. Whether you find yourself having to deal with children, neighbors, or coworkers, you will find the distinctions in this chapter a useful guide.

17 □

The highest rulers, people do not know they have them[1]
The next level, people love them and praise them
The next level, people fear them
The next level, people despise them[2]
If the rulers' trust is insufficient
Have no trust in them

Proceeding calmly, valuing their words
Task accomplished, matter settled
The people all say, "We did it naturally"[3]

1 The Tao always exists, so how can it fade away? This chapter isn't talking about the ever-present Tao of the universe, but the concept of it in our thoughts. When that concept fades away, we can no longer be congruent with the Tao in a natural way. We need concepts such as benevolence, compassion, justice, and righteousness to guide our actions and behavior.

2 The six family relationships are parent, child, older sibling, younger sibling, husband, and wife. When these six are in a state of harmony, the family enjoys a strong bond that requires no effort to maintain. When they degenerate into a state of disharmony, we must work on filial piety, obedience, and affection to keep the family together.

3 When a country descends into chaos and anarchy, it becomes crucial to make the distinction between ministers who are loyal and those who are not. In general, the further we stray from the harmony of the Tao, the more necessary it becomes to make distinctions. "Good" and "bad" end up so polarized that we tend to forget they emerged from the same Tao.

Think about what happens when hatred takes over your thoughts. Your antagonism against your enemy is so intense that it is impossible to see any common ground between the two of you. This harsh sense of separation is a sign that you have become too removed from the positive and uplifting Tao.

If it is possible for you to draw closer to the Tao, the hatred will begin to lose its grip. You gradually gain an ability to see things from the other person's perspective. Even if you cannot agree with that perspective, at least you begin to see the cause of the conflict. This is the beginning of understanding.

18

The great Tao fades away
There is benevolence and justice[1]
Intelligence comes forth
There is great deception

The six relations are not harmonious
There is filial piety and kind affection[2]
The country is in confused chaos
There are loyal ministers[3]

1 The character *jue*, translated as "end," means to discontinue. The concept is clear: we should put a stop to the obsession with book knowledge and focus on the wisdom of living outside of books. It is the ancient Chinese way of telling a bookworm to "get a life."

Some people have such a powerful desire for ever more knowledge that they fail to hear this message. They interpret "end" to mean "extreme" or "ultimate"; they change the first line to say that if one could gain the ultimate knowledge so that there is nothing more to learn, then people would benefit a hundredfold.

In this fashion, they have taken a warning against the blind pursuit of knowledge and transformed it into a rallying cry to acquire even more. The fact that this distortion can happen at all is the very reason Lao Tzu warns against it.

As we cultivate the Tao, let us keep Lao Tzu's admonition in mind. Knowledge isn't a bad thing per se, but book smarts can never replace street smarts, and school learning can never compare to life learning. We need both.

This is one of the most difficult chapters to understand, because we have a strong tendency to worship knowledge. We have all been conditioned to believe that knowledge is power, so how can having more be a bad thing?

Lao Tzu is unique among all the ancient philosophers in consistently highlighting the pitfalls of knowledge. In several chapters, including this one, he points to the link between intelligence and arrogance. He also points to the ease with which we can use knowledge in a shrewd way to twist the truth. In fact, this very chapter provides an excellent example.

19

End sagacity; abandon knowledge[1]
The people benefit a hundred times

End benevolence; abandon righteousness
The people return to piety and charity

End cunning; discard profit
Bandits and thieves no longer exist

These three things are superficial and insufficient
Thus this teaching has its place:
Show plainness; hold simplicity
Reduce selfishness; decrease desires

1 The blind pursuit of learning leads to excessive desires—the more you see, the more you want. Excessive desires, in turn, lead to anxiety and misery.

2 We tend to place too much importance on value judgments like good and evil. In reality, they are relative variables that change according to perspective.

3 Lao Tzu went about life with a healthy dose of caution. If people considered something to be bad, there was probably a reason for it, so he would proceed with care, even though he understood the relative nature of value judgments.

4 This is a reference to the vast gap between Tao cultivators and ordinary people. Lao Tzu uses it to describe himself as being far apart from others in many ways.

5 The infant represents the pureness of our *original nature*. In that state of grace, we see life as a marvel and look upon everything with a sense of wonder.

6 When Lao Tzu talks about not being overly calculating, he is specifically referring to our conduct in interpersonal relationships. Many people keep track of "scores"—slights, cold shoulders, backstabs—so when the time is right they can "even the score."

We have no need to do that. We take actions to protect ourselves from malicious people, but we otherwise let go of personal affronts without needing to retaliate in kind. People may think this is a severe disadvantage, but Tao cultivators see it very differently.

7 The first character in this line, *liao*, is translated as "high wind." It is a depiction of dynamic movement, to contrast with the tranquility of the calm seas.

8 The nourishing mother is a reference to the Tao, because the Tao is the source of life and provides for all living things.

20

Cease learning, no more worries[1]
Respectful response and scornful response
How much is the difference?
Goodness and evil
How much do they differ?[2]
What the people fear, I cannot be unafraid[3]

So desolate! How limitless it is![4]
The people are excited
As if enjoying a great feast
As if climbing up to the terrace in spring
I alone am quiet and uninvolved
Like an infant not yet smiling[5]
So weary, like having no place to return
The people all have surplus
While I alone seem lacking
I have the heart of a fool indeed—so ignorant!
Ordinary people are bright
I alone am muddled
Ordinary people are scrutinizing
I alone am obtuse[6]
Such tranquility, like the ocean
Such high wind, as if without limits[7]

The people all have goals
And I alone am stubborn and lowly
I alone am different from them
And value the nourishing mother[8]

1 "Indistinct" and "unclear" are used several times in this chapter. They refer to the mysteries of the Tao. We find the Great Unknown at the heart of existence. No matter how we probe it, total understanding eludes us. Every time we solve one puzzle, another presents itself.

2 One of the mysteries of the Tao is the essence of life. How exactly does life arise from inorganic—lifeless—material? This is something we still do not understand. How exactly did we—life forms not so different from others on this planet—become self-aware? This is another mystery that seems forever to remain just one step beyond comprehension.

3 The concept of the Tao originated well before the beginning of recorded history. It is far more ancient than most people realize. What is it about the Tao that gives it such lasting power? The only thing we can be sure of is that it is not a passing fad or a temporary fixation; it is the enduring and eternal truth.

Perhaps the answer to one of the mysteries above is that we are not life forms that have become self-aware. Perhaps it is the other way around: we are entities of pure consciousness that have learned how to manifest in the physical universe through the workings of life.

If this is true of us, then it is also true of the people around us. Let us put this idea to the test. When you interact with others, see them not as physical bodies, but as spiritual energy. How does this change the way you feel about them?

21

The appearance of great virtue
Follows only the Tao
The Tao, as a thing
Seems indistinct, seems unclear

So unclear, so indistinct
Within it there is image
So indistinct, so unclear[1]
Within it there is substance
So deep, so profound
Within it there is essence[2]

Its essence is supremely real
Within it there is faith
From ancient times to the present
Its name never departs[3]
To observe the source of all things
How do I know the nature of the source?
With this

1 The Chinese have a saying: "Take one step back. The ocean is wide; the sky is empty." What it teaches us is that when we yield in a potentially tense situation, we will suddenly feel a sense of wide open space—and wide open heart. Some may see yielding as a sign of weakness. Tao cultivators see it as a manifestation of courage and character, amply rewarded by wide open vistas.

2 Being low means being humble. To be filled is to receive abundantly. Just as lowly places tend to be filled with water, so too does a humble person receive an abundance of respect and goodwill.

3 This line highlights an interesting paradox. Sages have no wish to show off or be highly visible in any way. This makes them unique in a world where most people love to draw attention to themselves. Ironically, their uniqueness makes them conspicuous.

4 Like pliant plants, sages bend when the strong winds of contention blow. Because they do not get contentious or defensive, others cannot contend against them—there is literally nothing to attack.

5 Yielding in the Taoist sense does not mean suppressing the desire to fight. Instead, it means we relinquish the need to be defensive. Our views do not gain validity when we defend them, nor do they lose validity when we choose not to defend them. Therefore, being defensive amounts to nothing more than a tremendous waste of energy. Yielding lets us save this energy to be directed to something more constructive.

22

Yield and remain whole
Bend and remain straight[1]
Be low and become filled
Be worn out and become renewed
Have little and receive[2]
Have much and be confused
Therefore the sages hold to the one as an example for the world
Without flaunting themselves—and so are seen clearly[3]
Without presuming themselves—and so are distinguished
Without praising themselves—and so have merit
Without boasting about themselves—and so are lasting

Because they do not contend, the world cannot contend
     with them[4]
What the ancients called "the one who yields and
     remains whole"[5]
Were they speaking empty words?
Sincerity becoming whole, and returning to oneself

1 Tao cultivators value quality over quantity, and prefer fewer words with more meaning over many words with little meaning. Wind and rain (the words of nature) never last for too long. Therefore, measuring our words and saying more with less is an excellent way to emulate nature.

We should express ourselves in a concise manner and return to quietude once we have conveyed our meaning. We should also beware of people who claim to study the Tao and yet speak at great length in platitudes—they have no true understanding of this chapter.

2 These lines are a way to describe the law of cause and effect. The function of the Tao is indifferent and will let us reap what we sow. Whether it is the Tao, virtue, or loss, we become what we think about.

This means that we have the mandate to determine and direct our own thinking. Rather than allowing the mind to wander off in random directions, Tao cultivators impose discipline on themselves. Using fewer words is only the first stage in this discipline. It is followed by quiet introspection, where we consider our purpose in life and the best way to serve that purpose. Once we solidify our thoughts on this matter, our path (Tao) through life will become clear.

23

Sparse speech is natural
Thus strong wind does not last all morning
Sudden rain does not last all day
What makes this so? Heaven and Earth
Even Heaven and Earth cannot make it last
How can humans?[1]

Thus those who follow the Tao are with the Tao
Those who follow virtue are with virtue
Those who follow loss are with loss
Those who are with the Tao, the Tao is also pleased to
    have them
Those who are with virtue, virtue is also pleased to have them
Those who are with loss, loss is also pleased to have them[2]
Those who do not trust sufficiently, others have no trust in them

1 To stand on tiptoes is to raise oneself above others. This is an effective metaphor for arrogance, because we know from everyday experience that it is not possible to stand that way for long. Similarly, an arrogant person's façade of superiority cannot last.

2 To straddle is to strike an exaggerated pose. This represents pomposity—a pretentious display of the ego. Just as we cannot walk while straddling, so too can we not make any progress in life when we are too busy projecting a boastful sense of self-importance.

3 A common fallacy in the philosophical study of the Tao is the idea that because everything is relative and the Tao encompasses all, there are no "good" or "bad" things in the Tao. This chapter points out that true Tao cultivators regard arrogance as useless, harmful, and despicable. Although it is no less a part of the Tao than any other human trait, arrogance simply isn't something that can uplift and inspire most of us.

24 □

Those who are on tiptoes cannot stand[1]
Those who straddle cannot walk[2]
Those who flaunt themselves are not clear
Those who presume themselves are not distinguished
Those who praise themselves have no merit
Those who boast about themselves do not last

Those with the Tao call such things leftover food or tumors
They despise them
Thus, those who possesses the Tao do not engage in them[3]

1 We say that the Tao was born before Heaven and Earth because the principles that allowed for universal Creation are aspects of the Tao. Whether Creation is the result of Divine Will or the interaction of natural forces, it has to follow a certain set of rules. Therefore, the Tao had to exist before anything else.

The very fact that we exist is proof that the Tao must also exist. The paragraph you are reading now expresses an idea; that expression would not be possible without grammatical rules. Similarly, our existence is the physical expression written in the universal language of the Tao.

2 *Tao* is merely a name—really nothing more than a label. Ancient sages readily admitted that they knew little about it, but they could see that its function manifested in circular patterns everywhere, from a spherical raindrop to the majestic sweep of galaxies.

3 The sovereign is a natural leader who is congruent with the Tao. Such leaders can serve as examples for the people at any level of society.

The sovereign can also mean you, if you recognize your birthright to have absolute power over your life. As the owner of your destiny, you can direct it in any way you see fit. All you need is the realization and the willingness to aspire to greatness.

4 The cosmos is an orchestrated symphony on many levels. On Earth, human beings follow the laws of the land in which they live. The Earth itself follows the laws of astronomy—the rules that govern the motions of heavenly bodies. The universe as a whole follows the patterns of the Tao at the macroscopic level. Ultimately, the Tao itself follows natural laws, which arise from the Tao process, thus underscoring the self-completeness of the Tao.

There is something formlessly created
Born before Heaven and Earth
So silent! So ethereal!
Independent and changeless
Circulating and ceaseless
It can be regarded as the mother of the world[1]

I do not know its name
Identifying it, I call it *Tao*
Forced to describe it, I call it great
Great means passing
Passing means receding
Receding means returning[2]
Therefore the Tao is great
Heaven is great
Earth is great
The sovereign is also great[3]
There are four greats in the universe
And the sovereign occupies one of them
Humans follow the laws of Earth
Earth follows the laws of Heaven
Heaven follows the laws of Tao
Tao follows the laws of nature[4]

1 "Heaviness" here refers to the quality of gravitas in human affairs. Although Tao sages possess a gentle sense of humor, they are able to approach a situation with the appropriate degree of seriousness when necessary. This attribute is often associated with deliberation and dignity. "Lightness" is the opposite—a frivolous disregard for the matter at hand. In this context, it is often associated with restlessness and carelessness.

2 "Travel" here refers to the journey of life, and the heavy supplies are the essentials—the most important stuff, the basics. Sages are the ones who traverse through life without ever losing track of the fundamental essence that makes us human. Although there are many tempting sights of luxuries—the illusions of the material world that would distract us from the real goal—the sages remain unmoved.

3 "Ten thousand chariots" is a metaphor for great responsibility. In life, when we encounter a great responsibility, whether it's an important project at work or starting a family or anything else, we need to approach it with somber attitude and firm footing. Those who treat it lightly will be easily distracted and uprooted by the winds of adversity.

Heaviness is the root of lightness
Quietness is the master of restlessness[1]

Therefore the sages travel the entire day
Without leaving the heavy supplies
Even though there are luxurious sights
They are composed and transcend beyond[2]

How can the lords of ten thousand chariots
Apply themselves lightly to the world?
To be light is to lose one's root
To be restless is to lose one's mastery[3]

1 Skilled travelers in the journey of life follow the path of nature. They do not force their way through obstacles or trample over fellow travelers. They leave no signs of their passing. If we are similarly skillful in personal interactions, we would also follow the path of nature and not use words to find fault in others. To do so would be to leave unskillful skid marks all over the emotional landscape.

2 In ancient China, doors were locked from the inside with a wooden bar set horizontally. Thus, this line is talking about how we can capture people's attention so they naturally gravitate to us, as if they are locked in, but without the wooden bar. The key is to connect with them at a deep level, and form bonds that are stronger than any knots tied with ropes.

3 Sages do not give up on anyone. Everyone plays a role, and everyone has an impact. Good individuals can serve as teachers and examples for us. Not-so-good individuals are just as useful, because we can observe the consequences of their negative actions and learn what not to do.

4 This line describes the passing on of spiritual knowledge from one generation to the next. "Following enlightenment" means walking in the footsteps of past sages, to take their illuminating wisdom as our own. Some translators render the characters as "stealing light," which strays far from the original meaning.

5 Most of us do not value everyone equally. We develop likes and dislikes, preferences and aversions. We shower some with attention while ignoring others. We favor certain individuals while finding others barely tolerable. Most of us pay lip service to the concept of universal love, but few of us actually practice it. Lao Tzu would definitely see us as "greatly confused."

Good traveling does not leave tracks
Good speech does not seek faults[1]
Good reckoning does not use counters
Good closure needs no bar and yet cannot be opened
Good knot needs no rope and yet cannot be untied[2]

Therefore sages often save others
And so do not abandon anyone[3]
They often save things
And so do not abandon anything
This is called following enlightenment[4]

Therefore the good person is the teacher of the bad person
The bad person is the resource of the good person
Those who do not value their teachers
And do not love their resources
Although intelligent, they are greatly confused[5]
This is called the essential wonder

[1] Know the advantages of being forward and active, but keep to the principle of quietude and tranquility. We need both yin and yang to be truly complete.

[2] The watercourse of the world is a converging point, the nexus for the exchange of energy among people. To play this role, we need to know not only the importance of being dynamic and proactive but also how to handle people with courtesy and diplomacy.

[3] The state of the infant refers to the purity and simplicity of nature. We all manifested this state effortlessly when we were little, but the older we get, the further we stray from it.

[4] In this context, white means being highly visible, and black means being subtle. Sages understand the appropriate use of both.

[5] To be boundless means being able to move and act without being bound by limitations. Because we do not seek the limelight, we remain unknown while doing our work. Our anonymity lets us go where we are needed and do what needs to be done. This would not be the case if we drew attention to ourselves. One consequence of fame is the severe restriction in one's ability to go anywhere or do anything.

[6] We know what it is like to be highly regarded, but we hold to the principle of humility. We see ourselves as being with the common people, not above them. We become the valley to the world—we are open and receptive to the many diverse perspectives that people have.

[7] I translate *pu*, the most important character in this line, as "plain wood." It is often mistranslated as "uncarved block." *Pu* represents simplicity, plainness, and potentialities because a plain piece of wood has the potential to be carved into many different things.

28

Know the masculine, hold to the feminine[1]
Be the watercourse of the world
Being the watercourse of the world
The eternal virtue does not depart[2]
Return to the state of the infant[3]
Know the white, hold to the black[4]
Be the standard of the world
Being the standard of the world
The eternal virtue does not deviate
Return to the state of the boundless[5]
Know the honor, hold to the humility
Be the valley of the world[6]
Being the valley of the world
The eternal virtue shall be sufficient
Return to the state of plain wood
Plain wood splits, then becomes tools[7]
The sages utilize them
And then become leaders
Thus the greater whole is undivided

1 This view of the world as a sacred instrument dates back tens of thousands of years, long before the appearance of the term *Tao*. This common belief has been passed down by oral tradition in cultures throughout the world. As Native American spiritual traditions demonstrate, when we revere the sanctity of the world, we naturally feel a deep connection with nature and see ourselves as a part of it, not apart from it.

2 The Tao is all about balance. These descriptions depict the complementary balance that exists in nature, where different creatures play different roles, and all are necessary components in the interconnected web of ecology.

3 Creatures that have ownership are the ones that occupy their own environmental niche. Creatures that take by force are the predators who survive by hunting prey.

4 Let us emulate the natural balance of the Tao. Like the sages, we, too, can live in accordance with the principle of moderation. This chapter gives us three simple ways to behave: reduce extremes, avoid excess, and let go of arrogance.

29

Those who wish to take the world and control it
I see that they cannot succeed
The world is a sacred instrument
One cannot control it
The one who controls it will fail
The one who grasps it will lose[1]

Because all things:
Either lead or follow
Either blow hot or cold
Either have strength or weakness[2]
Either have ownership or take by force[3]

Therefore the sage:
Eliminates extremes
Eliminates excess
Eliminates arrogance[4]

1 This chapter expresses Lao Tzu's position against the military and violence in general. Those who are in tune with the Tao understand that violence begets more violence. Acts of aggression will inevitably cause retaliation and counterattack. This is as true between nations as it is between individuals.

2 The use of military power is, by its very nature, extremely negative. The thistles and thorns that flourish where the troops strike camp are symbolic of the negativity.

On a personal level, the camp represents the place in the heart where we harbor resentment and bitterness. The thorns represent the emotional poison that inevitably festers there.

3 This passage makes it clear that although Tao cultivators are against violence, they are not pacifists. They will do everything possible to avoid conflict, and yet remain ready and capable when backed into a corner.

Many of the greatest generals and martial artists in history were disciples of the Tao. They were dedicated to peace, but they were also devastating in combat. They used force only when they had no other choice, and once they achieved an intended result, they would go no further. To them, victory was not something to flaunt or even celebrate.

4 This observation from nature, that things grow strong and then age and perish, can be applied to the rise and fall of empires throughout history. Time and time again, ambitious nations become powerful, exert their will on other nations through force, and then decay from within. Empires never last, just as all things contrary to the Tao never last.

On a personal level, we can learn from this by living life with deliberate skill. Instead of aggression, we use courtesy; instead of heavy-handed tactics, we use a light touch; instead of forcing our will on others, we build consensus and harmonious teamwork.

30

The one who uses the Tao to advise the ruler
Does not dominate the world with soldiers
Such methods tend to be returned[1]

The place where the troops camp
Thistles and thorns grow[2]
Following the great army
There must be an inauspicious year

A good commander achieves result, then stops
And does not dare to reach for domination
Achieves result but does not brag
Achieves result but does not flaunt
Achieves result but is not arrogant
Achieves result but only out of necessity
Achieves result but does not dominate[3]

Things become strong and then get old
This is called contrary to the Tao
That which is contrary to the Tao soon ends[4]

1 This is a clear, uncompromising denouncement of the military. Lao Tzu wrote the Tao Te Ching when China was descending into the chaos of warfare, so chances are he observed its horrors firsthand.

2 The ancient Chinese observed that it was usually the right hand that wielded weapons, so they associated the right side with violence and the left with peace. This is quite different from the Western association of the right with goodness and the left with negativity (*sinister* is Latin for the left).

3 When forced to use the military, honorable individuals do so with detachment. They do not fight out of anger or hatred, and when they achieve victory, they do not consider it glorious.

4 Those who glorify war may think they have what it takes to conquer the world, but history shows they invariably fail to achieve their ambitions. They may dominate by force temporarily, but they never win the people's hearts.

5 With our understanding of how the ancient Chinese viewed left and right, we can easily decode this section. Auspicious events should be peaceful and harmonious, while inauspicious events are often linked with violence. The lieutenant general, responsible for the peacetime training of the military, is situated to the left of the emperor. The major general, responsible for leading attacks, is stationed to the right.

6 Because both generals represent the military, we regard them as if they are fixtures in a funeral. The term *funeral* in this context is also used as a generalized mourning for the many lives that are inevitably lost in battle. We grieve for these lives, no matter which side of the battle they fought on. We see the victory parade in the aftermath of war as a funeral march, no matter which side happens to be the victor.

31 □

A strong military, a tool of misfortune
All things detest it[1]
Therefore, those who possess the Tao avoid it
Honorable gentlemen, while at home, value the left
When deploying the military, value the right[2]

The military is a tool of misfortune
Not the tool of honorable gentlemen
When using it out of necessity
Calm detachment should be above all
Victorious but without glory[3]
Those who glorify
Are delighting in the killing
Those who delight in killing
Cannot achieve their ambitions upon the world[4]

Auspicious events favor the left
Inauspicious events favor the right
The lieutenant general is positioned to the left
The major general is positioned to the right[5]
We say that they are treated as if in a funeral
Those who have been killed
Should be mourned with sadness
Victory in war should be treated as a funeral[6]

1 To call the Tao nameless is to emphasize its eternal nature. The Tao was present long before there were humans around to name names; it will continue to be present after humans are gone and all the names have long been forgotten.

2 The sovereign can mean the emperor of China or a generic ruler. The latter can mean you, too, because you are the ruler of your inner kingdom. When the ancient emperor ruled China with the Tao, the people followed of their own accord; when you wield the Tao to govern your life, every aspect of it—mental, spiritual, physical—will also fall into line naturally.

3 "Sweet dew" is a metaphor for good fortune. Raining sweet dew means an abundance of good fortune. When we hold on to the Tao, everything seems to fall into place. Plans progress smoothly, people come to our aid, and things somehow work out in our favor more often than not. It is as if Heaven and Earth are actively helping us by granting us extra luck—thus the rain of sweet dew.

4 "Names" in this context is symbolic of complexity. The more complicated the world is, the more names we need to label everything. Complexity leads to chaos and conflicts. Stopping the increase of names means returning to the simplicity of the Tao.

5 This line is a recurring image in the Tao Te Ching: the streams in a valley flow together to form rivers and eventually pour into the ocean. This can represent all things returning to the Tao. It can also represent how we resonate powerfully with the Tao, and so gravitate toward it. In this chapter, it points to how naturally everything comes together for you when you are on the path of cultivation.

32

The Tao, eternally nameless[1]
Its simplicity, although imperceptible
Cannot be treated by the world as subservient

If the sovereign can hold on to it
All will follow by themselves[2]
Heaven and Earth, together in harmony
Will rain sweet dew[3]
People will not need to force it; it will adjust by itself

In the beginning, there were names
Names came to exist everywhere
One should know when to stop
Knowing when to stop, thus avoiding danger[4]

The existence of the Tao in the world
Is like streams in the valley flow into rivers and the ocean[5]

1 Tao cultivators recognize the great difficulty in knowing oneself. None of us can be very objective when it comes to self-assessment. Most of us are able to see others quite clearly, but ourselves not at all. This line is the Chinese equivalent of the ancient Greek maxim, *"Gnothi se auton"* or *"Know Thyself."*

2 To be powerful in this context means having authentic inner strength. This can be extremely difficult, because you are your own worst enemy. You know your vulnerabilities, and you know exactly how to take advantage of them.

This authentic inner strength is completely separate from external physical strength. An alcoholic who overcomes his addiction possesses true strength, even if he isn't much of a weight lifter.

3 This line refers to physical cultivation. Exercises such as *qigong* and tai chi can help us develop vitality and live life to the fullest. It is only through consistent, sustained practice that we can achieve results in a natural and healthy way. Therefore, the key to *qigong* and tai chi—and indeed any physical discipline—is willpower.

4 "Base" in this line refers to spiritual foundation. As we progress along the path of cultivation, it is a certainty that we will be tested over and over again. Those who have a solid foundation will withstand the trials; those who do not will be unable to handle the challenge.

5 To die and not perish means the memory of the deceased lives on. This, rather than the alchemical pursuit of immortality, is what we really mean by longevity. A noble goal for Tao cultivators is to live a life rich with meaning and full of the joy of helping others. Such a life continues on forever in the hearts of people—remembered, cherished, and missed.

33

Those who understand others are intelligent
Those who understand themselves are enlightened[1]

Those who overcome others have strength
Those who overcome themselves are powerful[2]

Those who know contentment are wealthy
Those who proceed vigorously have willpower[3]

Those who do not lose their base endure[4]
Those who die but do not perish have longevity[5]

1 Lao Tzu often uses water as a metaphor for the Tao. Here he takes the metaphor another level further, to bring in the aspect of *flow*. When water encounters an obstacle such as a rock, it does not attempt to destroy the obstacle. It simply flows around, over, or under it.

We can learn from this and apply it to life. When we encounter an obstacle, we may feel the urge to smash it, but the effort required to do that is not the best use of our energy. Instead, we should emulate water and simply find a way past it. There is always a way, as water demonstrates over and over again.

2 Just like water, we nurture other people without needing to take credit or exert influence over them. Water gives because that is its nature. Likewise, we give because it is natural for us. We attach no conditions, want nothing in return, and require no praise.

3 The Tao seems insignificant because it remains in the background. Its workings are subtle, imperceptible, and easy for most people to overlook. This seeming insignificance takes nothing away from its greatness. Despite its hidden nature, it is nevertheless the most fundamental force of reality. Although many people are not aware of it, none of us can exist without it. Thus, the Tao is insignificant and great at the same time.

4 The Tao is a transcendental force rather than a human-like entity. It has no human emotions and does not regard itself as the Lord of Creation or the Supreme Being. It goes about its business without elevating itself to a position of superiority. It has a basic humility that we observe and emulate, in order to act in accordance with the Tao.

34

The great Tao is like a flood
It can flow to the left or to the right[1]

The myriad things depend on it for life, but it never stops
It achieves its work, but does not take credit
It clothes and feeds myriad things, but does not rule over them[2]

Ever desiring nothing
It can be named insignificant
Myriad things return to it but it does not rule over them
It can be named great[3]

Even in the end, it does not regard itself as great
That is how it can achieve its greatness[4]

1 The image here means the concept of the Tao in the mind. To hold this image in the mind is to manifest a state of illuminated oneness, translucent clarity, and ineffable joy. People are naturally drawn to someone who can do this consistently.

2 Music and food represent all the physical pleasures of the material world. Lao Tzu compares them with the Tao in this and the following lines. The sound of music and the cooking smells attract the attention of passersby; the Tao attracts no attention to itself. The pleasures of the world delight the senses; the Tao is colorless and flavorless.

3 The Tao is not a pleasing picture, like a painting, because it cannot be seen. Nor is it a beautiful melody, like a song, because it cannot be heard. The Tao doesn't seem to offer much, but if we were to pause in our travels and investigate it in greater depth, we would discover something quite interesting. The enjoyment of music and food comes to an end sooner or later, but the function and utilization of the Tao goes on forever. Sensory pleasures are finite and transient, but the Tao is infinite and eternal—and so is the joy that one can discover within it.

35

Hold the great image
All under heaven will come[1]
They come without harm, in harmonious peace

Music and food, passing travelers stop
The Tao that is spoken out of the mouth
Is bland and without flavor[2]

Look at it, it cannot be seen
Listen to it, it cannot be heard
Use it, it cannot be exhausted[3]

1 The classical example of this process is "pride goeth before the fall." Consider what happens when a promising actor is surrounded by sycophants. They expand and strengthen his ego with endless flattery. He becomes disconnected from reality and believes he can do no wrong. Soon the bubble bursts and his projects collapse. His spectacular failures shrink and weaken his ego. In the meantime, another rising star assembles an entourage, and the process starts all over again.

2 This is especially true today. The massive consumerism of our society gives us numerous examples where certain things (gadgets, vehicles, movies, fashion, pop music, and so on) get hyped up to a fever pitch. After a while, the craze passes, and we move on to the next "in" thing. Yesterday's hits, bestsellers, and stars are thrown away and forgotten without a second thought.

3 In order to receive, first we must give. For instance, if we wish to be treated kindly, we must start by giving others loving-kindness. If we wish to make friends, we must start by being friendly. If we wish to be respected, we must start by respecting others. This works because the Tao process is circular; the principle underlying all interactions is one of dynamic, universal energy exchange.

4 The reason we call these insights subtle is that they seem to be contrary to our habitual thought patterns. To understand them is to become enlightened in the deeper workings of the Tao.

5 Not displaying sharp instruments here refers to the hidden nature of the Tao. The powerful insights of the sages can be used against people, but because it is our nature to nurture rather than harm others, we remain immersed in the benevolent Tao, like the fish keeping to the depths.

36

If one wishes to shrink it
One must first expand it
If one wishes to weaken it
One must first strengthen it[1]
If one wishes to discard it
One must first promote it[2]
If one wishes to seize it
One must first give it[3]
This is called subtle clarity[4]

The soft and weak overcome the tough and strong
Fish cannot leave the depths
The sharp instruments of the state
Cannot be shown to the people[5]

1 The Tao is both eternally devoid of action and the ultimate cause of all actions. It makes no attempt to achieve, and yet nothing is beyond its powers to achieve. It doesn't try to do anything; it simply does everything. Therefore, the Tao is the eternal, unchanging principle of effortless achievement. Within its workings there is no strife or struggle.

2 As it is in many other chapters, the sovereign here can be anything from the leader of a nation to the master of oneself. When we are able to hold the Tao and embody its principle of effortless achievement, everything around us—environment, circumstances, friends, family, relationships—will naturally transform into alignment with our goals.

3 When people are transformed into alignment with a leader, they may wish to move ahead with actions that, if unchecked, can lead to chaos. Similarly, those who become allies in our cause may do more harm than good out of a strong desire to take action. Our own thoughts and emotions, once aligned with a personal goal, can also get away from us out of sheer enthusiasm.

4 In these situations, we can restore balance by applying *pu*, the principle of plainness and simplicity. The fundamental nature of the nameless Tao is plain and simple. This total absence of contrivance and complexity lessens the urge to overreact and moderates desires.

37

The Tao is constant in nonaction
Yet there is nothing it does not do[1]

If the sovereign can hold on to this
All things shall transform themselves[2]
Transformed, yet wishing to achieve[3]
I shall restrain them with the simplicity of the nameless
The simplicity of the nameless
They shall be without desire
Without desire, using stillness
The world shall steady itself[4]

1 Those who have real virtue are not intentionally so; their actions are natural and unforced. Those who possess low virtue are not naturally virtuous, so they constantly have to remind themselves to act virtuously. Oftentimes, their actions advance specific personal agendas, such as improving their public image, assuaging guilty feelings, and so on.

2 Benevolence and righteousness are a bit different. Those who have the former contrive to act in benevolent ways, but because they do so out of compassion, their actions are free of personal agendas and attachments. Those who have the latter are also contrived, but because they feel so strongly justified in themselves, their actions always reflect their motives.

3 Etiquette is yet another step down from benevolence and righteousness. Those who have etiquette without the Tao act with contrived politeness and propriety. They fall back on protocol and rules to mask their true intentions, and if they fail to elicit from others the response they are looking for, they will use their arms—physical means—to force their views upon others in an aggressive manner.

4 In this context, "flowers of the Tao" is not a positive description. The basic idea is that flowers have a pleasing appearance but none of the satisfying goodness of fruits. Therefore, they are a metaphor for individuals who look good but lack substance. People who possess knowledge without real virtue fall into this category. They may project a knowledgeable image, but in fact they are ignorant in fundamental ways.

5 This is an admonition for us to focus on the inner essence instead of the veneer of superficiality. Instead of fussing over etiquette and knowledge, we should reach for benevolence, virtue … and finally the Tao.

38

High virtue is not virtuous
Therefore it has virtue
Low virtue never loses virtue
Therefore it has no virtue
High virtue takes no contrived action
And acts without agenda
Low virtue takes contrived action
And acts with agenda[1]
High benevolence takes contrived action
And acts without agenda
High righteousness takes contrived action
And acts with agenda[2]
High etiquette takes contrived action
And upon encountering no response
Uses arms to pull others[3]

Therefore, the Tao is lost, and then virtue
Virtue is lost, and then benevolence
Benevolence is lost, and then righteousness
Righteousness is lost, and then etiquette
Those who have etiquette
are a thin shell of loyalty and sincerity
And the beginning of chaos
Those with foreknowledge
Are the flowers of the Tao
And the beginning of ignorance[4]
Therefore the great person:
Abides in substance, and does not dwell on the thin shell
Abides in the real, and does not dwell on the flower
Thus they discard that and take this[5]

1 "Oneness" is a synonym for the Tao, because the Tao is the unifying principle at the core of everything. This oneness manifests itself not only in the external world but also in our inner selves. In fact, aspects of the external world reflect our internal world in highly specific ways. This is the key that will allow you to decode the following lines.

2 When we connect with the Tao, the oneness we attain gives us clarity in the mind, like the clear skies; tranquility in the heart, like the peaceful landscape; divine essence in spirituality, like the powerful gods; and abundant energy to live with zest, like the fertile valley overflowing with life.

3 Conversely, when we lack that connection, we experience the opposite. We struggle with confusion in the mind; we feel unsettled and ill at ease; the spiritual strength we enjoyed before has become an empty void; we are tired, listless, and unable to stir ourselves into action.

4 How can we lead with the Tao, if called upon to do so? The clues are everywhere. Nature shows us that the high must be built upon the low. The lower half of the mountain supports the upper half, and most of the mountain supports its majestic peak. It is the same in life: the highest honor must be built upon the lowest and most sincere form of humility.

5 This is why the sages never wish to shine brightly like gems. Instead, they prefer to be more like rocks, with only steadfast, solid consistency and no dazzling brilliance. This is also why the rulers of ancient China tended to use the lowliest terms to refer to themselves. Over time, the practice lost its meaning, but its original intent was very much congruent with the Tao.

39

Those that attained oneness since ancient times:[1]
The sky attained oneness and thus clarity
The earth attained oneness and thus tranquility
The gods attained oneness and thus divinity
The valley attained oneness and thus abundance
The myriad things attained oneness and thus life[2]
The rulers attained oneness and became the standard for
    the world
These all emerged from oneness

The sky, lacking clarity, would break apart
The earth, lacking tranquility, would erupt
The gods, lacking divinity, would vanish
The valley, lacking abundance, would wither
Myriad things, lacking life, would be extinct[3]
The rulers, lacking standard, would be toppled

Therefore, the honored uses the lowly as basis
The higher uses the lower as foundation[4]
Thus the rulers call themselves alone, bereft, and unworthy
Is this not using the lowly as basis? Is it not so?
Therefore, the ultimate honor is no honor

Do not wish to be shiny like jade
Be dull like rocks[5]

1 That which reverses course, reflects back, or returns to its point of origin characterizes the cyclical motions of the Tao. Because the Tao underlies everything in existence, we observe the same cyclical patterns everywhere.

2 "The weak" refers to things that exhibit flexible pliancy. They characterize the Tao because the Tao drives life forward. Living things are always soft and yielding; while dead things are stiff and unyielding.

This applies to the mind as well. An awareness that is in tune with the Tao is adaptable to new ways of thinking. In contrast, a mind that stubbornly clings to preconceptions and automatically rejects anything different is, in a real sense, already dead.

3 "Being" can also be translated as "existence"; "nonbeing" can be translated as "nonexistence." These lines describe how everything that has a tangible reality seems ultimately to come from nowhere.

Consider a tree. It is real; it has substance. It grew from a seed, which used to be inside a fruit, which came from the parent tree. The parent tree can trace itself back in time through the same process to its own parent. When we look back like this, we quickly get to a point where the tree, the seed, the fruit, and the parent tree had no existence and existed only as pure potentialities.

The same is true of us. When we trace our origin back in time, we will quickly realize that we, too, once existed as nothing more than possibilities. Thus, we must acknowledge that our being emerged from nonbeing.

This realization is the perfect antidote to worldly attachments. Next time you find yourself unable to let go, contemplate how we all came out of nothingness and must eventually return to it. When we understand this truth, we will see that our grasping ways make no sense at all.

40 ☐

The returning is the movement of the Tao[1]
The weak is the utilization of the Tao[2]

The myriad things of the world are born of being
Being is born of nonbeing[3]

1 Reaction to the Tao varies greatly, depending on the individual. Those who have achieved a higher level of understanding will resonate powerfully with the Tao when they encounter it. Those who are not quite there yet may not feel anything. Those who have yet to explore spirituality will simply fail to comprehend it.

2 This lack of comprehension often expresses itself as mockery. Such individuals laugh at the Tao because they feel the need to belittle that which is too unfamiliar to grasp easily. In their case, laughing is not a sign of happiness, but an attempt to disguise ignorance as a superior attitude.

Tao cultivators do not take offense at this. We understand that many people still live with the illusion of separateness—their world is black and white, us versus them, so anything beyond their comfort zone must be an enemy of sorts. Their lives are limited, so we do not regard them with annoyance or indignation, only with compassion and goodwill.

Sages liken such individuals to a frog who lives in a well. From its perspective at the bottom, the sky is rather small. If a bird were to stop by and tell it about the vast spaces outside, the frog would react with disbelief. Then, perhaps feeling a tinge of fear that it might be wrong, it would ridicule the bird, to drive it away, and along with it, the sense of discomfort.

The day will come when the frog grows strong enough to jump out of the well. Similarly, one day those who laugh at the Tao will gain enough spiritual maturity to venture beyond their limits. When that happens, they will see the wide open vistas for themselves, and they will know, in their heart of hearts, that nothing will ever be the same again.

41 □

Higher people hear of the Tao
They diligently practice it
Average people hear of the Tao
They sometimes keep it and sometimes lose it[1]
Lower people hear of the Tao
They laugh loudly at it
If they do not laugh, it would not be the Tao[2]

Therefore a proverb has the following:
The clear Tao appears unclear
The advancing Tao appears to retreat
The smooth Tao appears uneven
High virtue appears like a valley
Great integrity appears like disgrace
Encompassing virtue appears insufficient
Building virtue appears inactive
True substance appears inconstant
The great square has no corners
The great vessel is late in completion
The great music is imperceptible in sound
The great image has no form
The Tao is hidden and nameless
Yet it is only the Tao
That excels in giving and completing everything

1 In this line, the Tao is the pregnant void—an infinite field of nothingness bursting with potentialities. This formless, metaphysical Tao gives rise to the oneness that will eventually give rise to everything in the physical universe.

2 "One" represents the embryonic universe. As such, it begins with no opposites and no polarities, and then distills into yin and yang. Before anything else comes into existence, these two energies become distinct from one another. Thus, the oneness of the Tao gives rise to the two.

3 The two energies began to interact. They swirled into one another, neither one able to dominate or overwhelm its counterpart. A balance emerges from their interactions with one another. This is the critical third factor: movement, circulation, and rhythm, all embodied in the dynamic dance of yin and yang.

4 The dynamism between yin and yang produces everything. Life mirrors this in the interplay of male and female energies, resulting in reproduction. All living things are thus rooted in yin energy—the source of life—while moving to the rhythm of the active yang principle.

5 We are no exceptions to the above. The interaction of men and women perpetuates life and gives it meaning. This is important not only in terms of biology but spirituality as well. When we, as men and women, integrate the yin and yang energies, we achieve harmony and glimpse the divine nature of the Tao.

Another interpretation of this integration casts it in terms of our approach to life, rather than the interaction of the sexes. It says we should be grounded in the yin principle—humility, quietness, and tranquility—while embracing the yang principle—advancement, achievement, and progression.

42 □

Tao produces one[1]
One produces two[2]
Two produce three[3]
Three produce myriad things
Myriad things, backed by yin and embracing yang[4]
Achieve harmony by integrating their energy[5]
What the people dislike
Are alone, bereft, and unworthy
But the rulers call themselves with these terms

So with all things
Appear to take loss but benefit
Or receive benefit but lose
What the ancients taught
I will also teach
The violent one cannot have a natural death
I will use this as the principal of all teachings

1 I have translated the characters *chi cheng* as "override." This best represents the original meaning. The image evoked by these characters is a horseman riding a powerful, galloping steed. The rider cannot compare to the horse in terms of physical strength, but there is no question who is controlling whom. This is the perfect image for "the soft overcomes the hard."

2 Water seeps into and dissolves rocks; electricity flows through a block of metal. Thus, the intangible Tao can permeate all things, even if they appear to be solid, without any cracks or openings.

3 We can extrapolate from this to understand life. The Tao acts in a *wu wei* (unattached action) manner and effortlessly achieves the miracle of life. We find inspiration in this and see the possibility to act without attachments and achieve great works without friction or resistance.

4 We can teach most effectively through personal examples rather than preachy words. This is a function of the *wu wei* principle as well.

5 "Rarely matched" in this line has two interpretations. The first is that the power of the Tao is unmatched. The second is that the teachings of the Tao, as outlined in this chapter, are rarely matched by human intellect—or they are not well understood by most people.

43 □

The softest things of the world
Override the hardest things of the world[1]

That which has no substance
Enters into that which has no openings[2]

From this I know the benefits of unattached actions[3]
The teaching without words[4]

The benefits of actions without attachment
are rarely matched in the world[5]

1 If you feel the true self is more important than either fame or material possessions, is this feeling reflected in your daily actions? Do you pursue material things at the expense of spiritual cultivation, despite your conviction that the latter is more important?

2 For many people, this question has an obvious answer: decrease is always painful; increase is not so bad. Is this an accurate perception of reality? Is it a useful way to live life? Is it, in other words, in accordance with the Tao?

3 We have all seen how excessive love of material things compels one to spend. In our society, this spending is often done on credit, before we really have the financial resources to afford it. We have become a nation of debtors; every day we dig ourselves ever deeper.

4 We have seen the negative consequences of having too much. Our lives are filled with things that are not useful enough to keep, and yet not useless enough to discard. The clutter takes up space and denies us peace of mind. We worry about possible loss, theft, or damage. We cannot relax. Even before we actually lose anything, we have already lost a lot.

5 Therefore, the way of the Tao is contentment and being able to let go. Knowing when to stop is an important step—it prevents further accumulation of clutter. Being able to let go is the next step. There is a powerful feeling of liberation when we master this aspect of Tao cultivation.

Gain or loss, which is more painful? Once we experience the joy of simplifying and streamlining, we will understand that gain can bring unwanted complexity while loss can bring freedom. This understanding puts the question in a completely different light!

Fame or the self, which is dearer?
The self or wealth, which is greater?[1]
Gain or loss, which is more painful?[2]

Thus excessive love must lead to great spending[3]
Excessive hoarding must lead to heavy loss[4]

Knowing contentment avoids disgrace[5]
Knowing when to stop avoids danger
Thus one can endure indefinitely

1 "Great perfection" here can be read as a synonym for the Tao. "Flaw" in this context means a lack of completeness. This flaw that we may perceive in the Tao is due to our limited human perspective, as explained below.

2 Consider what happens when we observe people who have attained great mastery (perfection) in some aspect of life. It may have taken them years of hard work to refine their skills, but when we see them perform, they make everything look so easy. This is true whether they are Olympic gymnasts, world-class ballerinas, champion figure skaters, or others who work at the greatest level of human potential.

They achieve their effortless smoothness by completely integrating the techniques into their being. When we watch them, we see only the natural beauty of their self-expression; we do not see the rigidity of their rigorous training. Thus, at first glance, their great perfection may seem lacking—the techniques are nowhere to be seen—but as we continue to observe, we quickly realize that it is only because they have mastered the *ultimate technique of no technique*.

3 Similarly, those who have some speaking ability seem glib and verbose. They can carry on talking for hours, but the more they talk, the less they convince. The true masters, on the other hand, can express worlds of meaning with a few choice words. They may appear inarticulate to the uninformed, but in fact they possess the height of eloquence.

Test this teaching for yourself. Dedicate an entire day to the practice of minimal speech. Every time you want to say something, either say it with the fewest words possible or say nothing at all. Observe what happens. You may be surprised by how little you really need to talk.

45 □

Great perfection seems flawed[1]
Its function is without failure
Great fullness seems empty
Its function is without exhaustion

Great straightness seems bent
Great skill seems unrefined[2]
Great eloquence seems inarticulate[3]

Stillness overcomes movement
Cold overcomes heat
Clear quietness is the standard of the world

1 | When the world follows the Tao, harmony prevails. People know contentment and there is peace between nations. Because there is no war, fast horses no longer have a military function, so they are taken out of the army and redirected to till farmlands so farmers can then plant crops.

2 | When the world does not follow the Tao, strife prevails. People bicker among themselves, and nations clash endlessly. Because of constant warfare, all the horses are drafted into battle, so that even pregnant mares end up having to give birth on the battlefield.

These are among the most powerful and evocative images from the Tao Te Ching. The peaceful, pastoral scene of horses used for farming contrasts sharply with the misery and suffering of warfare.

3 | The driving force behind warfare and conflict is excessive desire at the expense of others. That is why there is no greater crime than greed, no greater disaster than not knowing when one has enough, and no greater fault than avarice, or covetousness. Conversely, the satisfaction we can derive from the feeling of contentment—at any level of material possession—is the true and lasting satisfaction. This is the peaceful bliss and self-sufficiency of those who follow the Tao.

46 □

When the world has the Tao
Fast horses are retired to fertilize the grounds[1]
When the world lacks the Tao
Warhorses must give birth on the battlefield[2]

There is no crime greater than greed
No disaster greater than discontentment
No fault greater than avarice
Thus the satisfaction of contentment
is the lasting satisfaction[3]

1 In ancient times, as today, many people thought they could become enlightened by traveling to places they considered sacred. They visited holy lands; they went on pilgrimages. Unlike them, Tao cultivators recognized that spirituality came from within, and so they did not feel the need to search frantically all over the material world for enlightenment.

2 We cannot comprehend the limitless Tao by looking through the limited view of a window. Sages turn their vision inward instead. Within our hearts there is an inner vision, which sees the world through the infinite perceptions of the Tao.

3 The knowing in the context of this line is an intuitive understanding, a direct interface with reality, one that is not dependent on the physical senses. It allows us to master wisdom no matter where we happen to be. It informs us that the Tao is not confined to any particular place, so there is no need for us to travel anywhere to gain mastery.

This chapter is sometimes misinterpreted as a teaching against travel, but as we have seen, what it really talks about is traveling for the purpose of gaining spiritual knowledge. As Tao cultivators, we prefer to stick to the original purpose of traveling—going places, seeing sights, and making friends.

47

Without going out the door, know the world[1]
Without peering out the window, see the Heavenly Tao[2]
The further one goes
The less one knows

Therefore the sage
Knows without going[3]
Names without seeing
Achieves without striving

1 Both gain and loss in this chapter refer to the complexity of life. When we pursue academic study, the increase of book knowledge leads to more complexity and ever-increasing desires. The more we know, the more we want.

2 The essence of the Tao is simplicity, so when we pursue the Tao, we reduce and discard the complexity in our lives. As we streamline and simplify, our desires will also decrease, and we discover that a simple and uncluttered life leads to peace and contentment.

3 "Unattached action" is my translation for *wu wei*, the state where we act without attachments to specific outcomes. I cannot use these characters directly in the translation, because, unlike the word *Tao*, they are not yet a formally recognized part of the English language.

4 The principle of *wu wei* is very powerful. By focusing on the process instead of the end result, we allow all things to progress naturally and minimize our tendency to meddle. The net effect is that the difficult becomes easy, and we struggle less but accomplish more.

5 "Take the world" in these two lines means achieving one's goals in the world. Those who do not understand *wu wei* may expend excessive resources, time, and energy toward achieving their goals, but end up with poor results. This is because they insist on asserting their manipulative influence, which makes everything more complex and therefore difficult to manage. They are so eager to achieve that they trip over themselves.

48

Pursue knowledge, daily gain[1]
Pursue Tao, daily loss[2]

Loss and more loss
Until one reaches unattached action[3]
With unattached action, there is nothing one cannot do[4]

Take the world by constantly applying noninterference
The one who interferes
is not qualified to take the world[5]

1 "Constant mind" means an inflexible and dogmatic way of thinking. It is a mindset that clings to certain beliefs, even in the presence of contrary evidence.

2 "The mind of the people" means multiple perspectives. As Tao cultivators, we never assume we are right. When our opinions differ from those of others, we examine alternative viewpoints carefully. This mindset is the opposite of dogma.

3 The compassion of the sages is truly universal. They treat people well, whether they are deserving of kindness or not. In general, sages expect the best from everyone and get it, because people cannot help but raise their standards to live up to the bar that the sages have set for them.

4 "The world" here means civilization. The sages are not hermits. They live among people, not far away from them. They feel true cultivation cannot be achieved in isolation, and they have a self-imposed obligation to care for the people.

Like the sages, we live fully immersed in modern life, with all of its noises and temptations. These distracting factors happen to be the perfect gauge for our spiritual progress. To be tested by them is why we come into the material world in the first place. If we go live on a mountain somewhere and distance ourselves from them, we defeat that very purpose.

49 □

The sages have no constant mind[1]
They take the mind of the people as their mind[2]
Those who are good, I am good to them
Those who are not good, I am also good to them
Thus the virtue of goodness
Those who believe, I believe them
Those who do not believe, I also believe them
Thus the virtue of belief[3]

The sages live in the world
They cautiously merge their mind for the world
The people all pay attention with their ears and eyes
The sages care for them as children[4]

1 The followers of life are the people who seek longevity and safety. They lead cautious lives with little risk or challenge. Their existence is usually uneventful and colorless.

Some translations render "three in ten" as one-third. This alters Lao Tzu's intended meaning. If Lao Tzu wanted to express one-third, he could have written "one in three."

2 The followers of death are the people with self-destructive tendencies. They rush headlong into any situation recklessly, and put their health and safety at risk.

3 The people in the third category start out living life to the fullest and sample all the pleasures of the world. It is easy to overindulge when they do this, so soon their excess takes a heavy toll on them. Overindulgence leads to death.

4 Nine persons out of ten fit into one of the three previous categories: fearful living, dangerous living, or excessive living. The rare exception, the one-in-ten minority, is the type who can transcend the predictable patterns that most people fall into.

Such people live in moderation; they do not shrink from the unfamiliar, but they are also not foolhardy. They are the skillful players—not spectators—in the game of life. They are fully engaged in their interactions with the world.

5 "The road" is the journey of life. Rhinos and tigers represent the hazards of daily existence, such as vicious rumors and criticisms. The army represents social competition. The weapons wielded by soldiers represent personal attacks. When we practice the art of living, none of these things can harm us.

6 Having "no place for death" means transcending fear, risk, and excess. If we can live this way, we will simply have no room for anything negative or destructive. We can achieve this by following Lao Tzu's recipe: practice moderation, use caution, and become an active participant in life.

50 □

Coming into life, entering death
The followers of life, three in ten[1]
The followers of death, three in ten[2]
Those whose lives are moved toward death
Also three in ten
Why? Because they live lives of excess[3]

I've heard of those who are good at cultivating life[4]
Traveling on the road, they do not encounter rhinos or tigers
Entering into an army, they are not harmed by weapons
Rhinos have nowhere to thrust their horns
Tigers have nowhere to clasp their claws
Soldiers have nowhere to lodge their blades[5]
Why? Because they have no place for death[6]

1 "Them" refers to all living things. "Virtue" in this context means the inherent power in everything. All living things grow and develop by virtue of the life force within them. Therefore, their "virtue" is their inherent power to live—an essential part of the Tao.

2 "Things" and "forces" refer to the tangible aspects of the environment. These aspects challenge all living things as they grow. If they survive the challenges, they become better adapted and more experienced.

3 This line points out that all living things have an inborn regard for the value of life within them. Indeed, they will fight to protect it at all costs. No one forced them to be this way; their instinct for self-preservation is as natural as their ability to breathe.

4 We, too, are part of nature. We, too, come from the Tao, the ultimate source. We are also shaped by our environment and tested by various forces. Although many may not be aware of it, we all learn, grow, and mature within the embrace of the Tao. The physical aspect of this growth happens automatically; the spiritual aspect of it is up to us.

5 We observe and emulate the Tao. This leads us to refrain from being possessive, immodest, and domineering.

6 It is because sages practice Mystic Virtue that they are so highly regarded. Just as all living things respect the Tao and treasure virtue, so too do the people who have received assistance, mentoring, or guidance from sages regard them with the highest respect and cherish the time spent with them. No one forced them to be this way; it is simply natural.

51

Tao produces them
Virtue raises them[1]
Things shape them
Forces perfect them[2]

Therefore all things respect the Tao and value virtue
The respect for Tao, the value of virtue
Not due to command but to constant nature[3]

Thus Tao produces them
Virtue raises them
Grows them, educates them
Perfects them, matures them
Nurtures them, protects them[4]

Produces but does not possess
Acts but does not flaunt
Nurtures but does not dominate[5]
This is called Mystic Virtue[6]

1 All effects can be traced back to causes, and when we trace the cause of everything back as far as we can, we arrive at the ultimate cause, the Tao. Thus, sages regard the Tao as the mother of all things.

2 The children of this mother are nothing less than *all of existence*. This includes us, so we, too, are the children of the Tao. When we realize that we come from this universal source and must eventually return to it, we begin to see reality more clearly. This clarity leads to greater understanding about life itself.

3 Knowing the Tao also leads one to a natural reduction of materialistic desires. Understanding of the Tao closes the doors and passages leading to temptations and distractions. This means one can easily focus on the task at hand and concentrate on cultivation.

As I also point out in chapter 56, the mouth is a major opening for temptations and distractions. It plays a central role in our various food and substance addictions; it is also where we unleash lies, vicious rumors, and intellectual sophistry. Those who cannot close the mouth are literally beyond help.

4 "Clarity" here means the ability to see things as they are, not as we wish them to be. In seeing things as they are, we understand the importance of details; we also understand how we can gain insights about the big picture from small things.

5 "Strength" in this context means inner strength, another defining characteristic of Tao cultivators. This strength does not manifest itself as physical force or an assertive personality, but as gentleness and kindness in dealing with others.

6 "Practicing constancy" is the application of discipline in our lives. Constant practice of the Tao involves repetitions and reminders, until the wisdom becomes second nature.

52

The world has a beginning
We regard it as the mother of the world[1]
Having its mother
We can know her children[2]
Knowing her children
Still holding on to the mother
Live without danger all through life

Close the mouth
Shut the doors
Live without toil all through life
Open the mouth
Meddle in the affairs
Live without salvation all through life[3]

Seeing details is called clarity[4]
Holding on to the soft is called strength[5]
Utilize the light
Return to the clarity
Leaving no disasters for the self
This is called practicing constancy[6]

1 In this chapter, we see the Tao as a path through life. The smartest thing we can do is to walk this path and not stray from it.

2 The path is wide, flat, and perfect for walking. This means the teachings of the Tao are plain, easy to understand, and easy to put into practice.

3 Traversing on the path of Tao is a gradual and steady process. Shortcuts seem appealing because they promise to save you time and effort. Their appeal is illusory, because sooner or later you'll realize that they all turn into detours or dead ends.

Sages note that great things are the accumulation of small, incremental steps. A tree grows a tiny amount every day until it becomes tall and strong. It offers passersby cool shade and perhaps even delicious fruits. It achieves these benefits without taking any shortcuts or using any quick fixes.

4 The corrupt court, barren fields, and empty warehouses are the result of people seeking shortcuts instead of walking the great Tao.

5 These descriptions depict the dishonest politician, a highly visible symbol of the degeneration that occurs when one strays far from the Tao. Corruption does not belong with the inspirational and uplifting Tao, so Lao Tzu emphatically declares that it isn't the Tao.

To be congruent with the Tao means to stay on course and make slow but steady progress toward the destination. This can only be accomplished one step after another. Each step does not seem like much, but over time all the steps add up to miles and miles of progress. We can use this insight to help us achieve great, long-term goals. The secret is consistent action sustained over a period of time.

53

If I have a little knowledge
Walking on the great Tao
I fear only to deviate from it[1]
The great Tao is broad and plain[2]
But people like the side paths[3]

The courts are corrupt
The fields are barren
The warehouses are empty[4]

Officials wear fineries
Carry sharp swords
Fill up on drinks and food
Acquire excessive wealth[5]

This is called robbery
It is not the Tao!

1 This chapter is about the permanence and strength of spirituality. If you plant the tree of wisdom deeply in the heart, it can never be uprooted. If you hold on to the virtues within, they can never be wrested away.

The material world is transient and impermanent. Anything physical, no matter how firmly grasped, can be taken from you. A fortress, no matter how strongly built, can be destroyed. Concepts, on the other hand, are not vulnerable to destruction. For instance, if a temple were demolished, the people could simply rebuild, because the idea still lives in their hearts. This single idea can manifest physical reality countless times. As long as there are people around who pass it on to others, the concept will remain eternally indestructible.

2 There are people who study the Tao for years and see no significant improvements in their lives. There are also those who walk the path for a relatively short time and yet experience dramatic and profound transformation. What accounts for the drastic difference?

The answer is cultivation. The Tao isn't just something to read or talk about; it is something to put into actual practice. Those who see the Tao only as a philosophy continue to live their lives as they always have, so nothing ever changes.

3 Tao cultivators see the Tao as a way of life. We are not content merely to play with ideas. We test the Tao by applying it to life. When we start seeing results in ourselves, we apply it to the family. When we have the loving and happy home we want, we extend the Tao into the community. Others see our happiness and become curious. Slowly but surely, we see the transformation of the Tao rippling outward.

54

That which is well established cannot be uprooted
That which is strongly held cannot be taken
The descendants will commemorate it forever[1]

Cultivate it in yourself; its virtue shall be true
Cultivate it in the family; its virtue shall be abundant
Cultivate it in the community; its virtue shall be lasting
Cultivate it in the country; its virtue shall be prosperous
Cultivate it in the world; its virtue shall be widespread[2]

Therefore observe others with yourself
Observe other families with your family
Observe other communities with your community
Observe other countries with your country
Observe the world with the world[3]
With what do I know the world?
With this

1 "Newborn infants" denotes a purer and simpler state of mind. It is a state full of bliss and grace. We all experienced it as babies, but we forget it as we grew up and became more and more affected by the material world.

2 Poisonous insects represent the sting of malicious gossip; wild beasts represent fear and anger; the birds of prey represent greed and envy. The Tao protects cultivators from these dangers, just like parents protect infants.

3 To be weak and soft in this context is to have a flexible and yielding approach. The firm grasp is an unwavering determination to reach one's goals. Together, these metaphors depict how we can be determined to achieve, and yet still remain flexible in our approach.

4 "Arousal" here refers to energy and vitality in living life with a sense of excitement, fun, and creativity.

5 Just as babies cry all day without getting hoarse, Tao cultivators who possess the optimum essence and harmony of health can concentrate on difficult tasks for an extended period of time without getting tired.

6 Both constancy and clarity refer to one's purpose. When we operate optimally, with our energies in perfect harmony with our surroundings, we begin to understand the meaning of life: Why are we here? What are we here to do?

7 Moderation is extremely important in this process. Tao cultivators do not cultivate physical vitality to excess, nor do they overtax the mind.

8 Think of life as a race. In this race, we are marathon runners, not sprinters. Sprinters may be able to surge forward in an explosive burst of speed, but within minutes their strength is depleted, and soon they collapse in a heap of exhaustion. Marathon runners are the ones who keep on going.

55

Those who hold an abundance of virtue
Are similar to newborn infants[1]
Poisonous insects do not sting them
Wild beasts do not claw them
Birds of prey do not attack them[2]
Their bones are weak, tendons are soft
But their grasp is firm[3]
They do not know of sexual union but can manifest arousal
Due to the optimum of essence[4]
They can cry the whole day and yet not be hoarse
Due to the optimum of harmony[5]
Knowing harmony is said to be constancy
Knowing constancy is said to be clarity[6]

Excessive vitality is said to be inauspicious
Mind overusing energy is said to be aggressive[7]
Things become strong and then grow old
This is called contrary to the Tao
That which is contrary to the Tao will soon perish[8]

1 This is the earliest form in history of "doers don't talk, talkers don't do" and "actions speak louder than words."

2 We recognize the mouth as a major source of trouble because of all the negative things that can come out of it: prejudice, slander, mockery … the list goes on.

3 The doors refer to the portals that lead to, or allow in, the many temptations and distractions of the material world.

4 "Sharpness" here refers to the sharp edge of arrogance. As compassionate Tao cultivators, we blunt this sharpness to avoid letting caustic and abrasive words hurt others.

5 The knots are the complexities of personal interactions. We use a light touch to unravel such knots and enjoy a simple, direct connection with fellow human beings.

6 The glare is the display of mental brilliance. Being naturally humble and full of self-effacing humor, we avoid showing off and thereby alienating people.

7 "Dust" is a metaphor for the material world. To mix in the material world means to be fully immersed in it. This means we do not set ourselves apart from the rest of humanity. We do not go into hermitage away from civilization, because the material world is where we can really put spiritual cultivation to the test.

8 People who possess Mystic Oneness can be fully involved with life and yet transcend it. We cannot influence them by getting close to them or treating them in a distant manner. It is equally useless to flatter them or attempt to pummel them into submission by degrading them. Such individuals are truly exceptional, and they invariably become honored by the entire world. Gandhi, Nelson Mandela, and the Dalai Lama are real-life examples of Mystic Oneness. This chapter is a very precise description of their character.

56

Those who know do not talk
Those who talk do not know[1]

Close the mouth[2]
Shut the doors[3]
Blunt the sharpness[4]
Unravel the knots[5]
Dim the glare[6]
Mix the dust[7]
This is called Mystic Oneness

They cannot obtain this and be closer
They cannot obtain this and be distant
They cannot obtain this and be benefited
They cannot obtain this and be harmed
They cannot obtain this and be valued
They cannot obtain this and be degraded
Therefore, they become honored by the world[8]

1 Ruling a country and using the military require two different methods. Using clever tactics to surprise the enemy is advantageous in that victory can be achieved with minimal loss of troops. Ruling a country is just the opposite—you wouldn't want to surprise your own people with clever tactics! Instead, you want to treat them with straightforward honesty.

2 Throughout history, sages have studied society and noted that the more regulations there are, the poorer people become. The ruler may wish to strengthen himself by keeping the people under control, but the poverty of the people erodes his power base, so he ends up weaker, not stronger.

3 In a restrictive and impoverished environment, many people turn to crime as a way to survive. They take up weapons to steal or rob; they also become increasingly tricky in their attempts to circumvent restrictions or exploit loopholes. Their cunning will often yield surprising and even bizarre results.

This national macrocosm mirrors the personal microcosm. Just as inept rulers confuse their subjects with excessive interference, so we, too, can meddle in our affairs or delude ourselves with false ideas.

4 Lao Tzu offers four practical suggestions as antidotes to the above problem. We, as rulers of our own little kingdoms, can: (1) take actions without attachments to specific outcomes; (2) quiet the mental chatter within before interacting with others; (3) do only what is necessary without interference; and (4) reduce and let go of excessive desires. These are time-tested ideas that work just as well for us as they did for the ancient rulers.

57

Govern a country with upright integrity
Deploy the military with surprise tactics[1]
Take the world with noninterference
How do I know this is so?
With the following:

When there are many restrictions in the world
The people become more impoverished[2]
When people have many sharp weapons
The country becomes more chaotic
When people have many clever tricks
More strange things occur
The more laws are posted
The more robbers and thieves there are[3]

Therefore the sage says:
I take unattached action, and the people transform themselves
I prefer quiet, and the people right themselves
I do not interfere, and the people enrich themselves
I have no desires, and the people simplify themselves[4]

1 "Lackluster" means without excessive interference—a government that respects individual rights and doesn't try to control people or invade their privacy. This way of governing allows us to live simply and honestly.

2 The opposite of the above is a government that monitors our every move. Such a government may appear to be capable and brutally effective, but because it burdens us with restrictions, it creates an environment where we are forced to become ever more evasive.

3 It is hard to say what is good or bad. A ruler may think it's a good thing to spy on people, without realizing that this leads to ever more dissatisfaction and alienation. What seems like a good idea can turn into a disaster and vice versa.

4 Because worldly affairs are so unpredictable, they can be very confusing for most of us. This is why sages recommend that we follow the Tao and not try to analyze every little detail. Logical analyses can yield the wrong conclusion, but the true Tao will never lead you astray.

5 To be scathing means to become self-righteous and condemn those who fail to live up to your standards.

6 To be piercing is to impose one's discipline of being incorruptible upon others. Sages do not do this—they are tough on themselves but tolerant toward everyone else. This makes perfect sense because we can always change ourselves but never others.

Therefore, discipline is most effective when we apply it in our own lives, and completely ineffective when we try to force it on other people, even if we start out with the best of intentions. The wisest thing we can do is give up trying to control others and focus energy on improving ourselves instead.

58 ☐

When governing is lackluster
The people are simple and honest[1]
When governing is scrutinizing
The people are shrewd and crafty[2]

Misfortune is what fortune depends upon
Fortune is where misfortune hides beneath
Who knows their ultimate end?
They have no determined outcome
Rightness reverts to become strange
Goodness reverts to become wicked[3]
The confusion of people
has lasted many long days[4]

Therefore the sages are:
Righteous without being scathing[5]
Incorruptible without being piercing[6]
Straightforward without being ruthless
Illuminated without being flashy

1 Conservation is the principle of valuing your time, energy, mind, and spirit. It is also the methodology of using them wisely and efficiently.

2 "Submitting" here means surrendering to the flow of the Tao. If the Tao is a river, then the idea is to give up moving against its currents. It is in our best interest to do so as soon as possible, because the sooner we stop wasting time and energy on activities contrary to the Tao, such as debates and intellectualizations, the sooner we can start accumulating positive virtues in life.

3 This is the path toward becoming a more authentic, powerful, and spiritual individual. Most of us tap into only a small fraction of the power we truly possess, so by directing your time, energy, mind, and spirit toward worthwhile cultivation, you become, literally, an unlimited individual.

4 To possess sovereignty is to gain power over yourself. It is also a natural authority that people respond to. You are able to influence them effortlessly because their respect for you flows naturally. Unlike the transient power achieved through force or domination, this is a positive force that lasts.

5 "Deep roots" and "firm foundation" both refer to the basis upon which we should build harmonious relationships with others. Such relationships are lasting and rewarding. We see them as an indispensable part of the Taoist life.

59

In governing people and serving Heaven
There is nothing like conservation[1]
Only with conservation is it called submitting early
Submitting early is called emphasis on accumulating virtues[2]
Accumulating virtues means there is nothing one
    cannot overcome
When there is nothing that one cannot overcome
One's limits are unknown[3]
The limitations being unknown, one can possess sovereignty
With this mother principle of power, one can be everlasting[4]
This is called deep roots and firm foundation[5]
The Tao of longevity and lasting vision

1 If you use too much heat, you will overcook the fish; if you keep turning the fish over and over, it will fall apart. Similarly, if a ruler constantly meddles in the affairs of the people with excessive rules and regulations, the country becomes chaotic and everyone suffers.

Similarly, when we manage our lives we also need to be careful not to second-guess ourselves too much. People who frequently change their minds (turn their decisions over) tend to fail in life.

2 The demons of negativity still exist, but they cannot exert their harmful influence. On a personal level, this means that when the Tao is present in your heart, your inner demons have no power over you.

3 This means the gods keep to their proper places and do not disrupt people's lives out of misguided benevolence. When we apply this concept to everyday cultivation, it means the wisdom of the Tao prevents us from taking foolish actions out of good intentions—actions that, although well-meaning, still end up making things more complicated and more difficult.

4 "Harming" in this context means meddling in people's lives. When we act in congruence with the Tao, we are able to relax, let things be, and simply enjoy the process.

5 "Returning" in this context means going back to the source, the Tao.

60

Ruling a large country is like cooking a small fish**¹**
Using the Tao to manage the world
Its demons have no power**²**
Not only do its demons have no power
Its gods do not harm people**³**

Not only do its gods not harm people
The sages also do not harm people**⁴**
They both do no harm to one another
So virtue merges and returns**⁵**

1 In this chapter, Lao Tzu points out that the virtue of humility applies not only to individuals and personal interactions but also to diplomacy and international relations. In fact, the microcosm of the personal reflects the macrocosm of the national, so principles that work on one level operate equally well on the other.

2 In the context of everyday living, the "large country" would be someone who has more power, while the "small country" would be someone with less. Because everything is relative, we are often called upon to play either role. For instance, a mid-level manager can be a "small country" to senior executives and at the same time be the "large country" to the rank and file.

3 "Lower position" means humility. The large country is more powerful and has a lot more resources than small countries do, but if it does not understand or practice the virtue of humility, it will quickly devolve from a well-respected world leader into a despised empire. History shows clearly that empires come and go, and when an empire falls, the smaller countries that used to cower at its feet will suddenly rise up against it.

4 When we apply this idea to the individual level, we see the wisdom of treating people well on one's way up, because it is indeed true that one will see all of them again on one's way down.

61

The large country is like the lowest river
The converging point of the world
The receptive female of the world
The female always overcomes the male with serenity
Using serenity as the lower position[1]

Thus if the large country is lower than the small country
Then it can take the small country
If the small country is lower than the large country
Then it can be taken by the large country[2]
Thus one uses the lower position to take
The other uses the lower position to be taken[3]
The large country only wishes to gather and protect people
The small country only wishes to join and serve people
So that both obtain what they wish
The larger one should assume the lower position[4]

1 These lines point out that the Tao provides for everyone, regardless of individual merits. Those who do not understand the Tao may not regard it as anything to value, but the Tao does not abandon them. It still provides for all the necessities people need to stay alive. Water, air, the sun … everything comes from the protective embrace of the Tao.

2 The most important ceremony in ancient China was the crowning of the Emperor and the installation of the three ministers. To emphasize its significance, the ceremony included offerings of jade and horses. The jade used was the largest and most valuable available; the horses were a team of four, each steed the fastest and finest in all of China.

3 The simple pleasure of sitting down with an open mind to get into the Tao surpasses any material riches. When we resonate deeply with a spiritual truth, when a teaching suddenly sheds light on a dilemma and liberates us from perplexing ignorance, that is when we realize the priceless nature of the Tao.

4 When the ancients searched for the answer to the ultimate question of life, they found it in the Tao. As for those who did not know enough to search, the Tao did not find fault with them. It gave them all the time they needed to work through their issues. With infinite patience, the Tao knew that one day, they, too, would embark on a spiritual quest of their own.

5 We are very fortunate to have so many options and so many opportunities to get to know the Tao. It is up to us to cherish it as the greatest treasure of all.

62 □

The Tao is the wonder of all things
The treasure of the kind person
The protection of the unkind person¹

Admirable words can win the public's respect
Admirable actions can improve people
Those who are unkind
How can they be abandoned?

Therefore, when crowning the Emperor
And installing the three ministers
Although there is the offering of jade before four horses²
None of it can compare to being seated in this Tao³

Why did the ancients value this Tao so much?
Is it not said that those who seek will find,
And those with guilt will not be faulted?⁴
Therefore, it is the greatest value in the world⁵

1 As Tao cultivators, we take proactive actions without attachments or expectations of specific outcomes. We manage processes and affairs without trying to manipulate them. We get a sense (a taste) of the situation without becoming so involved and engrossed that we lose our objectivity.

2 Whether tasks are great, small, many, or few, we approach them the same way. We treat everyone with the same degree of gentle kindness, so that even if someone attacks us out of anger or hatred, we do not fight fire with fire. Instead, we respond with compassion, against which there is no defense!

3 When handling a large or difficult task, we break it down into its constituent parts. If it is difficult, we start with its easiest part. If it is large, we start with its smallest component. These small and simple subtasks require little time and effort, and when they are complete, the success inherent in their completion generates positive energy. We then leverage this energy to catapult us toward the next smallest or easiest task. Each greater success generates greater energy, a greater feeling of satisfaction, and a greater ability to handle the next challenge.

4 This is how we achieve great and difficult tasks with ease. The secret is that we do not tackle such tasks head-on. To do so would be foolhardy and counterproductive.

5 Someone who makes promises quickly is likely to break them regularly. Therefore, Tao cultivators are reluctant to make overly optimistic projections in regard to a task at hand. Someone who thinks everything is easy is naive and inexperienced. Therefore, we regard all tasks as either challenging or potentially challenging. Whereas many people promise too much and deliver too little, we, like the Tao sages, promise little but deliver beyond expectations.

63 □

Act without action
Manage without meddling
Taste without tasting[1]
Great, small, many, few
Respond to hatred with virtue[2]

Plan difficult tasks through the simplest tasks
Achieve large tasks through the smallest tasks
The difficult tasks of the world
Must be handled through the simple tasks
The large tasks of the world
Must be handled through the small tasks[3]
Therefore, sages never attempt great deeds all through life
Thus they can achieve greatness[4]

One who makes promises lightly must deserve little trust
One who sees many easy tasks must encounter much difficulty
Therefore, sages regard things as difficult
So they never encounter difficulties all through life[5]

1 It is relatively easy to maintain a situation when everything is peaceful and quiet. When the possibility for chaos is nearly nonexistent, it is simple to keep everything in check. Generally speaking, it is always easier to act on something effectively when it is small. It's best to nip a potential problem in the bud so it doesn't get the chance to grow into something serious.

2 This same principle extends to many aspects of life. The mightiest trees started as a small shoot, barely noticeable in the ground. The tallest building had to be built from the ground up. There was a time when it was nothing more than a pile of dirt brought to the site in preparation for construction to begin.

3 The greatest, most epic journey you can undertake still must begin where you stand. Similarly, great deeds can have a small, indeed humble, beginning. When we keep this great wisdom in mind, it becomes easier for us to overcome inertia and take that first step.

The ancient Chinese measurement of distance, *li*, is loosely translated as "mile." One *li* is about half a kilometer, and roughly a third of a mile.

Many people know the expression, "A journey of a thousand miles begins with one step." They may not know that it originally came from this chapter. Some may be aware that the saying is Chinese in origin, but mistakenly attribute it to Confucius. Another interesting thing to note is that the popular expression is, in fact, a mistranslation. The original contains no character for "one" or "step." What it really says is that the little piece of ground beneath your feet is the starting point of a long journey, just like tall trees and great buildings have small beginnings.

64

When it is peaceful, it is easy to maintain
When it shows no signs, it is easy to plan
When it is fragile, it is easy to break
When it is small, it is easy to scatter
Act on it when it has not yet begun
Treat it when it is not yet chaotic[1]
A tree thick enough to embrace
Grows from the tiny sapling
A tower of nine levels
Starts from the dirt heap[2]
A journey of a thousand miles
Begins beneath the feet[3]

The one who meddles will fail
The one who grasps will lose
Therefore, sages do not meddle and thus do not fail
They do not grasp and thus do not lose

People, in handling affairs
Often come close to completion and fail
If they are as careful in the end as the beginning
Then they would have no failure

Therefore, sages desire not to desire
They do not value goods that are hard to acquire
They learn to unlearn
To redeem the fault of the people
To assist the nature of all things
Without daring to meddle

1 The sage kings of ancient China used the Tao to guide people toward simplicity rather than cleverness and knowledge. They did so because they understood that cleverness and knowledge would bring desires and deceit, which would in turn lead to complexities and chaos, thus making things more difficult for everyone.

2 These kings never used guile and manipulation to govern. Doing so causes great harm to the country—really not so different than stealing from it like a thief. On the other hand, guiding everyone toward simplicity leads to benefits for all and is a great blessing to the country.

3 Both of these approaches—shrewd cunning versus straightforward plainness—are "standards," and it is important to know both. The ancient masters made it a point to understand Machiavellian methods thoroughly, while embracing upright, honest simplicity in actual practice. This mindset of never losing sight of both is known as Mystic Virtue.

4 The power of Mystic Virtue is beyond measure. It is both profound in its implications and far-reaching in its effectiveness. It runs counter to the tendency to pursue material things, and opposite the desire for short-term gains. We see it as achieving a state of great congruence, because Mystic Virtue follows nature and is therefore perfectly in tune with the Tao.

Think of your life as a sovereign state, and yourself as the ruler. If, like many people, you run your life with cleverness and contrived craftiness, you will also make things more complex and difficult to manage. A complicated life filled with tension and stress is one where joy has been taken away—by none other than yourself. You would thus be the thief who robs your own life of happiness.

65

Those of ancient times who were adept at the Tao
Used it not to make people brighter
But to keep them simple
The difficulty in governing people
Is due to their excessive cleverness[1]
Therefore, using cleverness to govern the state
Is being a thief of the state
Not using cleverness to govern the state
Is being a blessing of the state[2]

Know that these two are both standards
Always knowing these standards
Is called Mystic Virtue[3]
Mystic Virtue is so profound, so far-reaching
It goes opposite to material things
Then it reaches great congruence[4]

1 Rivers and oceans receive everything from the streams and rivulets of a hundred valleys. It is as if they are the rulers, and the valleys are the loyal subjects who pay tributes into the royal treasury. The reason for this is simple: rivers and oceans occupy the lower positions, so all the streams and rivulets naturally flow into them.

2 The principle applies equally well to human interactions. If we wish to win friends and influence people, we must also occupy the lower positions, just as rivers and oceans do. This means being truly humble.

True humility compels us to place ourselves behind others out of the wish to be of service. This is actually the essence of true leadership, which is not about ordering people around, but about serving the greater good.

3 As leaders, sages utilize the Tao rather than force or domination. People assist them voluntarily, without coercion or pressure. Although the position of a sage appears to be above the followers, people do not feel burdened or oppressed.

We can follow the same principles in building relationships and promoting harmony, so that people naturally align with us and do not resent our authority. In fact, they may even push us to accept the mantle of power, knowing that we can be trusted with the responsibility.

4 This is a very different concept from the conventional "might makes right" paradigm, where one seizes power by force and bullies others with it. The sages are the exact opposite. By following their example, we, too, will receive abundantly and enjoy the support of people, who follow the leadership of the Tao from the heart, willingly and gladly.

66 □

Rivers and oceans can be the kings of a hundred valleys
Because of their goodness in staying low
So they can be the kings of a hundred valleys[1]
Thus if sages wish to be over people
They must speak humbly to them
If they wish to be in front of people
They must place themselves behind them[2]
Thus the sages are positioned above
But the people do not feel burdened
They are positioned in front
But the people do not feel harmed
Thus the world is glad to push them forward
        without resentment[3]
Because they do not contend
So the world cannot contend with them[4]

1 The Tao is an infinite concept that has no form, substance, limit, or boundaries. If it were finite, then no matter how big it is, there would always be something far bigger that dwarfs it.

2 Compassion means our loving-kindness toward all things; conservation means knowing when to avoid wasting our time and energy, and instead direct them in a meaningful way, in accordance with our purpose in life; not daring to be foremost in the world means humility, the awareness that seeing ourselves as above others can only lead to failure.

3 True courage doesn't come from macho posturing or false bravado. Rather, we gain true courage from love and a commitment to something greater than ourselves.

4 By having humility, we can connect with the Tao of leadership. Within this Tao, we lead without focusing on ourselves, without wanting to be the center of attention. We concentrate on what needs to be done and let others shine.

5 All three treasures are important, and we must use them together. Courage without compassion is nothing more than brutality. To reach widely without conserving our resources quickly leads to exhaustion. Forgetting the lesson of humility, becoming arrogant, and letting the ego run wild are the beginning of self-delusion.

6 If we can hold on to the three treasures, we can achieve extraordinary results. When we fight with compassion in our hearts, we can achieve victory, because love gives us strength. Because we follow the Tao, events will seem to conspire in rendering assistance at just the right time, as if we are safeguarded by divine powers. All manner of resources and allies will rally to our cause, in unexpected ways that no one could foresee. Such is the power of the Tao.

67

Everyone in the world calls my Tao great
As if it is beyond compare
It is only because of its greatness
That it seems beyond compare
If it can be compared
It would already be insignificant long ago[1]

I have three treasures
I hold on to them and protect them
The first is called compassion
The second is called conservation
The third is called not daring to be ahead in the world[2]
Compassionate, thus able to have courage[3]
Conserving, thus able to reach widely
Not daring to be ahead in the world
Thus able to assume leadership[4]
Now if one has courage but discards compassion
Reaches widely but discards conservation
Goes ahead but discards being behind
Then death![5]
If one fights with compassion, then victory
With defense, then security
Heaven shall save them[6]
And with compassion guard them

1 As Sun Tzu remarks, the greatest warrior is the one who wins without fighting. In the battlefields of life, are we great generals or warriors? Do we get aggressive with people? Do we get angry easily? If so, then we cannot claim greatness.

Lao Tzu suggests that the better way is for us to approach the battle with calmness and composure. This increases our effectiveness in action and allows us to achieve victory with a minimum of fighting, or no fighting at all.

2 To lower oneself is to be humble. Because skillful managers are not arrogant in assuming that they are more capable than everyone else, they are able to delegate authority and empower others to utilize their talents fully.

3 Non-contention applies not only to military leadership but also to social interactions. It is a powerful way to manage our personal relationships with other people. If we follow this virtue at the workplace, we will be at peace with coworkers. We will not get angry with them or engage them in petty squabbles. This virtue leads not only to harmony but also to success.

4 "Heaven" means nature, which is always non-contentious. In a thunderstorm we can sense tremendous power, but no hatred, anger, or arrogance. When the ancient sages noted this, they made non-contention their ultimate principle.

68 ☐

The great generals are not warlike
The great warriors do not get angry
Those who are good at defeating enemies do not engage them[1]
Those who are good at managing people lower themselves[2]
It is called the virtue of non-contention
It is called the power of managing people[3]
It is called being harmonious with Heaven
The ultimate principle of the ancients[4]

1 In this saying, the host is the aggressor, who, by advancing too eagerly into battle, is likely to become overextended and unbalanced. The guest is the cautious defender who retreats to allow the aggressor to stumble and thus defeat himself.

In the host-guest dynamic, the ancient Chinese see the host as the active party, who urges visitors to sit, drink, and eat. The guest is the passive one, who reacts to the actions initiated by the host.

2 Lao Tzu compares life strategy to military strategy. In life, as in war, we should advance purposefully with a plan (march in formation), take definite actions (move our arms), come to grips with the problem (grapple with the enemy), and bring effective tools to bear (utilize weapons). In this comparison, underestimating one's enemy is equivalent to underestimating one's challenges in life. This often causes us to charge forth recklessly and get blindsided; we become the eager host and forget to be the cautious guest.

3 Many people believe that overwhelming aggression wins respect. This belief forms the basis of the "shock and awe" military strategy. History shows that it simply does not work. Aggression succeeds only in planting the seeds of subsequent retaliation. It is wisdom and restraint that win respect and admiration, not force.

Judo and aikido are based on the concepts described in this chapter. A master of these arts may appear to be yielding and retreating, and yet is devastatingly effective in combat. Tao sages apply the same approach to life. Acting from compassion, they realize that it is more important to be kind than to be right. When you find yourself in an argument, why not yield and let the other party win? What do you really have to "lose"?

69 □

In using the military, there is a saying:
I dare not be the host, but prefer to be the guest[1]
I dare not advance an inch, but prefer to withdraw a foot

This is called marching in formation without formation
Raising arms without arms
Grappling enemies without enemies
Holding weapons without weapons
There is no greater disaster than to underestimate the enemy
Underestimating the enemy almost made me lose my treasures[2]

So when evenly matched armies meet
The side that is compassionate shall win[3]

1 Although Lao Tzu's teachings are simple and based on universal truths, we may fail to understand and practice them. This is because many of us are looking for something that is flashy and conspicuous; something that costs money and therefore must be valuable; and something that works magically without requiring disciplined effort. The Tao is none of these things, so we may look at it, lose interest, and move on to something else.

2 Those who do understand the Tao are rare and exceptional individuals. When we join the ranks of such individuals, our actions are true to our words and thoughts; we excel quietly, invisibly, and unknown to most. People may misunderstand us, because, like the sages, we assume an unremarkable appearance while holding spiritual treasures deep in the heart.

70

My words are easy to understand, easy to practice
The world cannot understand, cannot practice
My words have basis
My actions have principle
People do not understand this
Therefore they do not understand me[1]
Those who understand me are few
Thus I am highly valued
Therefore the sage wears plain clothes but holds jade[2]

1 "To know that you do not know" means recognizing your own ignorance. This is a good thing, because it motivates you to continue seeking answers and keeps you from becoming presumptuous and arrogant. The opposite of this is being ignorant but assuming that you possess knowledge. This is a flaw that many of us have.

☲ In this chapter, I translate the character *bing* as "fault" or "flaw." Many translators translate it as "disease" or "illness" instead, which is the dictionary definition as well as the common usage, but in this case it doesn't quite fit.

When Lao Tzu uses *bing*, he is specifically referencing human errors and character flaws—being sick or defective in some aspect of one's thinking. This context still exists in modern Chinese. For instance, when we say *mao bing*, we are talking specifically about a fault or a problem.

2 It is only when we see a problem clearly, and recognize that we need to do something about it, that we can begin to free ourselves of it.

3 Sages are human, too, and they make mistakes just like everyone else. What makes them different is that they look at themselves with the clarity of detachment, whereas most of us are blind to our own faults. Because they are naturally humble, sages do not automatically assume they must be correct. When they recognize that they have made a mistake or manifested a problem, they take action to address the issue.

4 People who know that they do not know and take steps to learn will eventually acquire the knowledge they need. Similarly, if we can monitor ourselves, recognize our faults, and work on correcting them, we will ultimately rid ourselves of them.

71

To know that you do not know is highest
To not know but think you know is flawed[1]

Only when one recognizes the fault as a fault
can one be without fault[2]

The sages are without fault
Because they recognize the fault as a fault[3]
That is why they are without fault[4]

1 Sages have observed that everything in nature reaches an extreme and then reverses course, like the swing of a pendulum. It is the same with people. When they no longer fear the dominating force of authority, they will bring about greater force against the authority in an uprising.

2 Wise rulers advocate freedom. They do not attempt to limit the people in their thoughts and actions, nor do they interfere with the people's means of livelihood. To do otherwise is to oppress the people, which will invariably result in the people's rejection of authority.

When we apply this concept to ourselves, it becomes obvious that this chapter is talking about denying and suppressing ourselves. When we keep emotions bottled up for too long, they reach an extreme and reverse course. This is why self-denial and suppression are rarely the best ways to manage life.

3 Sages see the uprising of the people against an arrogant ruler as a cautionary tale: If we possess the clarity of self-knowledge, we do not need to put ourselves on a pedestal and seek external validation. If we possess the confidence of self-respect, we do not need to praise ourselves or highlight our own achievements.

72 ☐

When people no longer fear force
They bring about greater force[1]

Do not limit their place
Do not reject their livelihood
Because the ruler does not reject them
Therefore they do not reject the ruler[2]

Therefore the sages:
Know themselves but do not glorify themselves
Respect themselves but do not praise themselves[3]
Thus they discard that and take this

1 Here we have an interesting distinction between courage and daring. Courage means being resolute and firm. Daring means throwing caution to the wind—full speed ahead and damn the torpedoes. The former is an inner quality borne of conviction; the latter is an external display of braggadocio.

2 These two approaches yield different results. The careful resolve brings benefits, while the reckless charge brings harm. It is as if Heaven dislikes those who are rash and punishes them accordingly.

3 Perhaps this is due to the nature of the Heavenly Tao. We can see that the Tao contends with no one, and yet wins out in the end. If we possess courage in the Taoist sense, then we, too, can achieve our objectives in the long run without being contentious.

The Tao is silent, and yet instantaneously responsive. In the same way, we, too, can be quiet while remaining sensitive to external conditions. When things change, we are ready to alter our approach, quietly and efficiently.

The Tao manifests itself in everything. Taking our cue from this, we are also fully present in our activities. By being aware and mindful of the here and now, we enhance and deepen everything we do.

The Tao is never rushed, and yet its infinite organizing power coordinates every event in the cosmos. If we possess courage in accordance with the Tao, then we, too, can be unhurried and well prepared. We take our time in thoughtful planning, so we can act with composure and maximize our chances of success.

4 The Tao is like a net that stretches across the cosmos. This matrix of existence is loose and relaxed, and yet it takes everything into account and does not leave anything out. Those who possess courage act in harmony within this net, and therefore appear to be favored by Heaven.

73 □

The bold in daring will be killed
The bold in not daring will survive¹

Of these two, one may benefit, the other may harm
The one hated by Heaven²—who knows the reason?
Even the sages still find this difficult

The Tao of Heaven:
Does not contend and yet excels in winning
Does not speak and yet excels in responding
Is not summoned and yet comes on its own
Is unhurried and yet excels in planning³
The heavenly net is vast
Loose, and yet does not let anything slip through⁴

1 Capital punishment was a fact of life in ancient China. The sages observed this and noted that the practice did not seem very effective as a deterrent. Criminals still existed, as if they had no fear of death.

2 There is an ever-present master executioner. Call it karma, or the law of reciprocity, or the law of cause and effect. This executioner is perfectly impartial and never fails to dispense the appropriate punishment, including death.

The concept of the "master executioner" in this chapter mirrors the "heavenly net" concept from the previous chapter. They are different ways of describing the same karmic mechanism that seems to pervade reality.

3 There is no need for us to assume the role of this master executioner, to enact what we perceive to be justice. Trying to do so is similar to beginners trying to cut wood like an expert carpenter. When they fumble around with sharp tools, they are likely to accidentally cut themselves. Similarly, if we kill on behalf of the master executioner, we are likely to harm ourselves. In other words, a society that avidly supports capital punishment in a bloodthirsty way is not doing itself any favors.

Aside from the observation that the death penalty doesn't seem effective as a deterrent, we should also consider the possibility that innocents may be executed by mistake—and certainly those who are killed can no longer make amends and repay their debt to society.

The central idea in this chapter is that the negative approach is rarely effective. Capital punishment does not necessarily improve society. If we execute everyone on death row today, we will feel no safer tomorrow. The more we resort to killing as a response to our frustration and anger toward violence, the more violent society becomes.

74

People do not fear death[1]
How can they be threatened with death?
If people are made to constantly fear death
Then those who act unlawfully
I can capture and kill them
Who would dare?
There exists a master executioner that kills[2]
If we substitute for the master executioner to kill
It is like substituting for the great carpenter to cut
Those who substitute for the great carpenter to cut
It is rare that they do not hurt their own hands[3]

1 When people are hungry, it is because the ruler overzealously imposes ever-increasing taxes, leaving very little for them to sustain themselves. Similarly, when we feel spiritually empty, it can be because we have overtaxed ourselves and neglected our basic spiritual needs. Overextended and mentally exhausted, we forget to feed the soul with inspirational sustenance.

2 When people are difficult to control, it is because the ruler is constantly meddling by imposing many restrictive rules. In reaction, the people become defiant against authority. In the same way, when we meddle in other people's business, life becomes more difficult to manage. Our excessive interference makes everything complicated. Our friends become alienated, and our relationships become strained and distant.

3 When people disregard death, it is because the ruler pursues an extravagant lifestyle, indulging in ever more luxuries while people suffer hardship. When they see this, the people brave death to rise against the ruler.

When the mind is overly greedy in pursuing materialistic indulgences, the spirit suffers. Life becomes an endless series of sensory stimulations, devoid of meaning. It no longer seems worthwhile, and makes us wonder: Why bother? Why go on?

4 To strive for living means to pursue luxuries obsessively. A wise ruler does not do this. Under such a ruler, the people do not starve (their basic needs are met), they are not difficult to govern (they gladly follow leadership), and they have no reckless disregard for death (their lives are worth living).

As the emperor of your own life, you have a responsibility to be a wise ruler. That means paying attention to your spiritual needs and simplifying your life. If you have a tendency to meddle, you need to let go. Spend some time cherishing life instead—it is too amazing a gift to be wasted on other people's business.

75

The people's hunger
Is due to the excess of their ruler's taxation
So they starve[1]
The people's difficulty in being governed
Is due to the meddling of their ruler
So they are difficult to govern[2]
The people's disregard for death
Is due to the glut in their ruler's pursuit of life
So they disregard death[3]
Therefore those who do not strive for living
Are better than those who value living[4]

1 Living things are characterized by softness and pliancy; death is characterized by dryness and rigidity. We can see this just by looking around. When plants and animals are dead, their lifeless forms lose all trace of moisture and therefore all flexibility and suppleness.

2 Thus, being yielding and flexible is the way to embrace life. By keeping this in mind, our approach to life becomes dynamic and capable of growth and adaptation. When changes occur, we can handle the challenge. We can thrive in a world of constant change, while those who are inflexible encounter increasing difficulties and resistance.

3 An army that cannot adapt to the ever-changing conditions on the battlefield will soon find itself outmaneuvered and defeated by an enemy that is more nimble. A tree that grows hard and strong makes excellent timber, and so will quickly be chopped down and put to use. These are both examples where rigidity leads to death.

4 That which is forceful and aggressive may seem to have the upper hand, but in fact occupies a lower position of disadvantage. Conversely, being yielding and flexible may be perceived as a weakness, but is in fact a great strength that occupies a higher position, leading to victory and success.

Again, this Tao principle pervades all aspects of life. Therefore, companies that use high-pressure sales tactics will not end up with the most satisfied customers and repeat business. Similarly, if we apply pressure to others in an attempt to make them do what we want, we will end up with resentment and alienation.

Smart companies apply no pressure. They provide attention, service, and assistance to customers, thus earning their trust, which can lead to repeat business and referrals. If we use the soft approach in life, we, too, can win the trust of others—and end up with happy customers of our own!

76

While alive, the body is soft and pliant
When dead, it is hard and rigid
All living things, grass and trees,
While alive, are soft and supple
When dead, become dry and brittle[1]
Thus that which is hard and stiff
is the follower of death
That which is soft and yielding
is the follower of life[2]
Therefore, an inflexible army will not win
A strong tree will be cut down[3]
The big and forceful occupy a lowly position
While the soft and pliant occupy a higher place[4]

1 The workings of the Tao can be compared to archery. If the arrow is pointing too low or too high, we must compensate by tilting up or down. The amount of strength that goes into pulling back the bowstring also has to be just right, or the arrow will either overshoot the target or fall short.

The above is sometimes mistranslated as being the adjustments in the length of the bowstring when making a bow. To understand what Lao Tzu is really saying, we need to look at the chapter as a whole. It should be quite clear that the art of archery is a metaphor for *hitting the target* in life.

2 The Tao acts in a balanced way. It tends to reduce whatever is too much, and add to that which is insufficient. Thus, everything in the world is constantly moving toward equilibrium. A pot of hot water, if left alone, will gradually cool off. Just as certainly, ice cubes taken out of the freezer will melt.

3 People often act in ways opposite to the balancing principle of the Tao. They cut down that which is already lacking and give to that which already has too much. They despise the impoverished while heaping praise upon the rich and powerful. They ignore the needy while focusing attention on celebrities.

4 We can keep the Tao in mind and not follow the herd. Whenever we have too much of anything, we can offer the surplus to those who do not have enough. In this fashion, we give in the same way that nature does—without claiming credit or feeling superior or the need to show off. It makes no difference whether people never find out about the good we have done. Having the Tao is its own reward.

77

The Tao of Heaven
Is like drawing a bow
Lower that which is high
Raise that which is low
Reduce that which has excess
Add to that which has deficiency[1]

The Tao of Heaven
Reduces the excessive
And adds to the deficient[2]

The Tao of people is not so
Reducing the deficient
In order to offer to the excessive[3]

Who can offer their excess to the world?
Only those who have the Tao
Therefore, sages act without conceit
Achieve without claiming credit
They do not wish to display their virtue[4]

1 Water appears to be the weakest and softest thing in the world. It always conforms to the shape of its container. Pour it into a bottle, it's a bottle; pour it into a cup, it's a cup. Water is the ultimate symbol of the yielding and flexible aspect of the Tao.

2 At the same time, there is also nothing better than water at dissolving the hardest and most unyielding rocks. We only have to look around to see how water has carved ravines and canyons out of mountains all over the world. Water is the universal solvent. Nothing can replace it.

3 This observation of water teaches us that despite a yielding, humble appearance, the weak overcomes the strong and the soft overcomes the hard. This is a principle that we can all understand, yet somehow we cannot put it into practice in real life. We still have a tendency to meet force with force. When someone yells at us, we yell back louder; when someone trespasses against us, we retaliate in full measure.

4 How should we react to humiliation? To accept it calmly requires far more strength of character than to respond with hostility and aggression. Remember the power of water, and let it guide you to yield … and overcome.

5 What happens when we encounter misfortune? If we can be like water, then we, too, will have the depth of character to contain difficulties and disappointments. Keep the lesson of water with you as you handle setbacks in your life.

6 By embracing the seemingly weak and soft, we gain personal power. This is a truth that, at first glance, appears contrary to expectations!

78

Nothing in the world is softer or weaker than water[1]
Yet nothing is better at overcoming the hard and strong
This is because nothing can replace it[2]

That the weak overcomes the strong
And the soft overcomes the hard
Everybody in the world knows
But cannot put into practice[3]

Therefore, sages say:
The one who accepts the humiliation of the state[4]
Is called its master
The one who accepts the misfortune of the state[5]
Becomes king of the world
The truth seems like the opposite[6]

1 It doesn't matter how we say "no hard feelings." After a bitter dispute, there's bound to be residual ill will.

2 Sages give without expecting anything in return. It is as if they hold the left part of the lending agreement but do not demand payments from the borrower. The "left part" means the lender's copy. It refers to the ancient Chinese method of keeping track of debts, which existed even before the invention of paper. Lender and borrower would take a piece of wood or tree bark and carve a record of their transaction on it. Then they would split it down the middle. The left part would go to the lender; the right to the borrower.

The left part was the lender's proof of his right to demand payments. When the loan was fully paid, the lender would give the left part to the borrower, thus making the contract whole. The restored contract then became the borrower's proof that he had fulfilled his obligations. Because the tear was uneven, it served as the perfect and natural way to authenticate the contract. A forged left side will never match the right side—a simple and brilliant solution!

3 Tax collectors take from everyone and give to no one. Unlike them, Tao cultivators hold the left half of the contract. This means that we give without expecting anything in return. When we do that, the Tao sees to it that we are amply rewarded, despite the complete lack of expectations.

4 How can it be that generous souls prosper while misers are forever pinching pennies? Shouldn't those who take from others end up with more than those who give? It is not because the Tao plays favorites. It is because the law of cause and effect ensures that those who give in accordance with the Tao will receive abundantly.

79

After settling a great dispute
There must be remaining resentments[1]
How can this be considered good?
Therefore, the sage holds the left part of the contract
But does not demand payment from the other person[2]
Those who have virtue hold the contract
Those without virtue hold the collections[3]

The Heavenly Tao has no favorites
It constantly gives to the kind people[4]

1 This chapter is about an ideal place where people have vehicles and weapons but do not need to use them. It reflects the time when the Tao Te Ching was written—a time of strife, with many refugees displaced by armed conflicts. It is unfortunate that these lines also reflect the world today. In some ways, humanity has not made much progress in the 2,500 years since Lao Tzu's time.

2 "Tying knots" was a way for people to record events. It is a general metaphor for simple solutions, which are often the most effective and reliable solutions.

3 Food need not be elaborate to be delicious; clothes need not be extravagant to be comfortable. We can use this as an inspiration for simplifying our lives. Do we absolutely need luxuries to be happy?

4 To be able to hear your neighbors' roosters and dogs means you do not live far away from them. Despite the close proximity, there is no friction. People in an ideal community do not bicker.

What can we do if we are in a place with much bickering? We can start by embracing peace and letting go of the need to get back at someone who has wronged us. The transformation from contention to harmony has to begin somewhere; we may as well be the first to move toward the ideal place described in this chapter.

The last line is often misunderstood. Some think it means people in this land do not visit one another. This isn't quite right, because Tao cultivators are hardly antisocial. When we take the meaning of the entire chapter into consideration, it becomes clear that the last line really means people do not *visit trouble* upon one another. In this ideal place, petty games of tit for tat simply do not exist.

80

Small country, few people
Let them have many weapons but not use them
Let the people regard death seriously
And not migrate far away

Although they have boats and chariots
They have no need to take them
Although they have armors and weapons
They have no need to display them[1]

Let the people return to tying knots and using them[2]
Savor their food, admire their clothes[3]
Content in their homes, happy in their customs

Neighboring countries see one another
Hear the sounds of roosters and dogs from one another
The people, until they grow old and die
Do not go back and forth with one another[4]

1 These lines can sometimes be misused. People who like to criticize others may cite these words to justify their behavior. The difference between them and sages lies in intention. Sages speak plainly and truthfully when doing so benefits others without harming them.

2 Those who are skillful in the art of living recognize the futility of arguments and refrain from engaging in debates. Sages let actions reveal their virtues; they have no need to explain themselves with words.

Sometimes we think we are helping friends by arguing with them, but because this brings contention into the relationship, it can do more harm than good. People are rarely at their best when a debate causes them to become defensive and stubborn. It would be better for us to leave the matter alone, and wait for the right time to approach the subject.

3 When we say "jack of all trades, master of none," we are describing people who have not achieved excellence in any one thing. It is as if they are digging many shallow wells and not getting much water. The opposite is someone with true mastery of knowledge, someone who has no wish to chase after a broad spectrum of subjects. When we align ourselves with this concept, we concentrate only on a few wells, digging them deeply and getting as much water as we want.

4 "Accumulate" refers to worldly goods. We do not need to pursue the accumulation of goods because we can find contentment and abundance in helping and giving. The more we render assistance, the more joyous fulfillment we feel; the more we give, the more we receive.

5 The positive, uplifting Tao of Heaven benefits all things. The rain waters all plants; the sun warms everyone. In emulating this, we also seek to benefit all people and refrain from hurting them with criticism or contention.

81

True words are not beautiful
Beautiful words are not true[1]
Those who are good do not debate
Those who debate are not good[2]
Those who know are not broad of knowledge
Those who are broad of knowledge do not know[3]

Sages do not accumulate
The more they assist others, the more they possess
The more they give to others, the more they gain[4]

The Tao of Heaven
Benefits and does not harm
The Tao of sages
Assists and does not contend[5]

Notes ☐

1. Michael Crichton's answers to the Amazon.com Significant Seven quiz, accessed January 17, 2011, www.amazon.com/gp/product/0066214130/ 104-0551459-5998326?v=glance&n=283155.
2. Eckhart Tolle, *A New Earth: Awakening to Your Life's Purpose* (New York: Dutton/Penguin Group, 2005).
3. Tao Te Ching, background information on Wikipedia.org, accessed January 17, 2011, en.wikipedia.org/wiki/Tao_Te_Ching.

Acknowledgments ☐

"Drink water, think of the source" is a Chinese saying that reminds us never to forget those who brought us into the world. In honor of this sentiment, I would like to acknowledge first and foremost Kim T. Lin and Jenny Lin, for the gift of life, nurture, and Chinese culture.

In the same vein, I must also acknowledge Wu Han Yih and Lin Hsiu Mei for setting the ultimate example of living life in complete accordance with the Tao. They are an inexhaustible source of inspiration.

The accuracy and authenticity of this book come from the teachings of Master Mong Ying, Grand Master Yuen Zhu Uh, and Grand Master Lin De Yang. These real-world sages of the I-Kuan Tao tradition personify the Tao with every word and action. This book is a testimonial to their matchless understanding of Lao Tzu and the Tao Te Ching.

I am truly fortunate to have received so much assistance from so many special individuals. Chief among them is Mark Ogilbee, whose editing skills and natural affinity to the Tao have extracted better work from me than I ever imagined possible.

I am grateful to the members of the English Study Group at the Great Tao Foundation, who have provided me with valuable feedback in my Tao Te Ching lectures every Sunday for the past ten years. I am equally grateful to the friends of the www.taoism.net website, who have supported my cause and kept me going since its inception in 1998. Some of these wonderful friends, including Becca James and Richard Seymour, have gone far beyond the norm in giving of themselves.

Finally, this book is dedicated to Janice Lin, the one person who makes everything possible. She holds the key that opens the door to all wonders.

Suggestions for Further Reading ☐

Capra, Fritjof. *The Tao of Physics: An Exploration of the Parallels between Modern Physics and Eastern Mysticism.* 5th ed. Boston: Shambhala Publications, 2010 .

Chopra, Deepak. *The Seven Spiritual Laws of Success: A Practical Guide to the Fulfillment of Your Dreams.* San Rafael, CA: Amber-Allen Publishing, 1995.

Chung, Tsai Chi. *The Tao Speaks: Lao Tzu's Whispers of Wisdom.* New York: Anchor Books/Doubleday, 1995.

———. *Zhuangzi Speaks: The Music of Nature.* Princeton, NJ: Princeton University Press, 1992.

Deng, Ming-Dao. *365 Tao: Daily Meditations.* San Francisco: HarperSanFrancisco, 1992.

———. *Everyday Tao: Living with Balance and Harmony.* San Francisco: HarperSanFrancisco, 1996.

Merton, Thomas. *The Way of Chuang Tzu.* New York: New Directions, 1965.

Watts, Alan. *Tao: The Watercourse Way.* New York: Pantheon Books, 1975.

———. *What Is Tao?* Novato, CA: New World Library, 2000.

Please visit me online at www.taoism.net. I have designed the website to be the perfect complement to this book. It offers the following:

- In-depth analyses of passages and characters
- Stories to illustrate the teachings of the Tao
- Insights about applying the Tao to life

The website also hosts a forum for Tao cultivators from all over the world. Please consider this book your personal invitation to join this community!

Spiritual Practice

Fly Fishing—The Sacred Art: Casting a Fly as a Spiritual Practice
by Rabbi Eric Eisenkramer and Rev. Michael Attas, MD
Illuminates what fly fishing can teach you about reflection, awe and wonder; the benefits of solitude; the blessing of community and the search for the Divine.
5½ x 8½, 192 pp (est), Quality PB, 978-1-59473-299-7 **$16.99**

Lectio Divina—The Sacred Art: Transforming Words & Images into Heart-Centered Prayer *by Christine Valters Paintner, PhD*
Expands the practice of sacred reading beyond scriptural texts and makes it accessible in contemporary life. 5½ x 8½, 192 pp (est), Quality PB, 978-1-59473-300-0 **$16.99**

Haiku—The Sacred Art: A Spiritual Practice in Three Lines
by Margaret D. McGee 5½ x 8½, 192 pp, Quality PB, 978-1-59473-269-0 **$16.99**

Dance—The Sacred Art: The Joy of Movement as a Spiritual Practice
by Cynthia Winton-Henry 5½ x 8½, 224 pp, Quality PB, 978-1-59473-268-3 **$16.99**

Spiritual Adventures in the Snow: Skiing & Snowboarding as Renewal for Your Soul *by Dr. Marcia McFee and Rev. Karen Foster; Foreword by Paul Arthur*
5½ x 8½, 208 pp, Quality PB, 978-1-59473-270-6 **$16.99**

Divining the Body: Reclaim the Holiness of Your Physical Self *by Jan Phillips*
8 x 8, 256 pp, Quality PB, 978-1-59473-080-1 **$16.99**

Everyday Herbs in Spiritual Life: A Guide to Many Practices
by Michael J. Caduto; Foreword by Rosemary Gladstar
7 x 9, 208 pp, 20+ b/w illus., Quality PB, 978-1-59473-174-7 **$16.99**

Giving—The Sacred Art: Creating a Lifestyle of Generosity
by Lauren Tyler Wright 5½ x 8½, 208 pp, Quality PB, 978-1-59473-224-9 **$16.99**

Hospitality—The Sacred Art: Discovering the Hidden Spiritual Power of Invitation and Welcome *by Rev. Nanette Sawyer; Foreword by Rev. Dirk Ficca*
5½ x 8½, 208 pp, Quality PB, 978-1-59473-228-7 **$16.99**

Labyrinths from the Outside In: Walking to Spiritual Insight—A Beginner's Guide
by Donna Schaper and Carole Ann Camp
6 x 9, 208 pp, b/w illus. and photos, Quality PB, 978-1-893361-18-8 **$16.95**

Practicing the Sacred Art of Listening: A Guide to Enrich Your Relationships and Kindle Your Spiritual Life *by Kay Lindahl* 8 x 8, 176 pp, Quality PB, 978-1-893361-85-0 **$16.95**

Recovery—The Sacred Art: The Twelve Steps as Spiritual Practice *by Rami Shapiro; Foreword by Joan Borysenko, PhD* 5½ x 8½, 240 pp, Quality PB, 978-1-59473-259-1 **$16.99**

Running—The Sacred Art: Preparing to Practice *by Dr. Warren A. Kay; Foreword by Kristin Armstrong* 5½ x 8½, 160 pp, Quality PB, 978-1-59473-227-0 **$16.99**

The Sacred Art of Chant: Preparing to Practice
by Ana Hernández 5½ x 8½, 192 pp, Quality PB, 978-1-59473-036-8 **$15.99**

The Sacred Art of Fasting: Preparing to Practice
by Thomas Ryan, CSP 5½ x 8½, 192 pp, Quality PB, 978-1-59473-078-8 **$15.99**

The Sacred Art of Forgiveness: Forgiving Ourselves and Others through God's Grace
by Marcia Ford 8 x 8, 176 pp, Quality PB, 978-1-59473-175-4 **$18.99**

The Sacred Art of Listening: Forty Reflections for Cultivating a Spiritual Practice
by Kay Lindahl; Illus. by Amy Schnapper 8 x 8, 160 pp, b/w illus., Quality PB, 978-1-893361-44-7 **$16.99**

The Sacred Art of Lovingkindness: Preparing to Practice
by Rabbi Rami Shapiro; Foreword by Marcia Ford 5½ x 8½, 176 pp, Quality PB, 978-1-59473-151-8 **$16.99**

Sacred Attention: A Spiritual Practice for Finding God in the Moment
by Margaret D. McGee 6 x 9, 144 pp, Quality PB, 978-1-59473-291-1 **$16.99**

Soul Fire: Accessing Your Creativity
by Thomas Ryan, CSP 6 x 9, 160 pp, Quality PB, 978-1-59473-243-0 **$16.99**

Thanking & Blessing—The Sacred Art: Spiritual Vitality through Gratefulness
by Jay Marshall, PhD; Foreword by Philip Gulley 5½ x 8½, 176 pp, Quality PB, 978-1-59473-231-7 **$16.99**

Spirituality

The Heartbeat of God: Finding the Sacred in the Middle of Everything
by Katharine Jefferts Schori; Foreword by Joan Chittister, OSB
Explores our connections to other people, to other nations and with the environment through the lens of faith. 6 x 9, 240 pp, HC, 978-1-59473-292-8 **$21.99**

A Dangerous Dozen: Twelve Christians Who Threatened the Status Quo but Taught Us to Live Like Jesus
by the Rev. Canon C. K. Robertson, PhD; Foreword by Archbishop Desmond Tutu
Profiles twelve visionary men and women who challenged society and showed the world a different way of living. 6 x 9, 160 pp (est), Quality PB, 978-1-59473-298-0 **$16.99**

Decision Making & Spiritual Discernment: The Sacred Art of Finding Your Way *by Nancy L. Bieber*
Presents three essential aspects of Spirit-led decision making: willingness, attentiveness and responsiveness. 5½ x 8½, 208 pp, Quality PB, 978-1-59473-289-8 **$16.99**

Laugh Your Way to Grace: Reclaiming the Spiritual Power of Humor
by Rev. Susan Sparks A powerful, humorous case for laughter as a spiritual, healing path. 6 x 9, 176 pp, Quality PB, 978-1-59473-280-5 **$16.99**

Living into Hope: A Call to Spiritual Action for Such a Time as This
by Rev. Dr. Joan Brown Campbell; Foreword by Karen Armstrong
A visionary minister speaks out on the pressing issues that face us today, offering inspiration and challenge. 6 x 9, 208 pp, HC, 978-1-59473-283-6 **$21.99**

Claiming Earth as Common Ground: The Ecological Crisis through the Lens of Faith
by Andrea Cohen-Kiener; Foreword by Rev. Sally Bingham
6 x 9, 192 pp, Quality PB, 978-1-59473-261-4 **$16.99**

Bread, Body, Spirit: Finding the Sacred in Food
Edited and with Introductions by Alice Peck 6 x 9, 224 pp, Quality PB, 978-1-59473-242-3 **$19.99**

Creating a Spiritual Retirement: A Guide to the Unseen Possibilities in Our Lives
by Molly Srode 6 x 9, 208 pp, b/w photos, Quality PB, 978-1-59473-050-4 **$14.99**

Creative Aging: Rethinking Retirement and Non-Retirement in a Changing World
by Marjory Zoet Bankson 6 x 9, 160 pp, Quality PB, 978-1-59473-281-2 **$16.99**

Keeping Spiritual Balance as We Grow Older: More than 65 Creative Ways to Use Purpose, Prayer, and the Power of Spirit to Build a Meaningful Retirement
by Molly and Bernie Srode 8 x 8, 224 pp, Quality PB, 978-1-59473-042-9 **$16.99**

Hearing the Call across Traditions: Readings on Faith and Service
Edited by Adam Davis; Foreword by Eboo Patel
6 x 9, 352 pp, Quality PB, 978-1-59473-303-1 **$18.99**; HC, 978-1-59473-264-5 **$29.99**

Honoring Motherhood: Prayers, Ceremonies & Blessings
Edited and with Introductions by Lynn L. Caruso 5 x 7¼, 272 pp, HC, 978-1-59473-239-3 **$19.99**

Journeys of Simplicity: Traveling Light with Thomas Merton, Bashō, Edward Abbey, Annie Dillard & Others *by Philip Harnden*
5 x 7¼, 144 pp, Quality PB, 978-1-59473-181-5 **$12.99**; 128 pp, HC, 978-1-893361-76-8 **$16.95**

The Losses of Our Lives: The Sacred Gifts of Renewal in Everyday Loss
by Dr. Nancy Copeland-Payton 6 x 9, 192 pp, HC, 978-1-59473-271-3 **$19.99**

Renewal in the Wilderness: A Spiritual Guide to Connecting with God in the Natural World *by John Lionberger*
6 x 9, 176 pp, b/w photos, Quality PB, 978-1-59473-219-5 **$16.99**

Soul Fire: Accessing Your Creativity
by Thomas Ryan, CSP 6 x 9, 160 pp, Quality PB, 978-1-59473-243-0 **$16.99**

A Spirituality for Brokenness: Discovering Your Deepest Self in Difficult Times
by Terry Taylor 6 x 9, 176 pp, Quality PB, 978-1-59473-229-4 **$16.99**

A Walk with Four Spiritual Guides: Krishna, Buddha, Jesus, and Ramakrishna
by Andrew Harvey 5½ x 8½, 192 pp, b/w photos & illus., Quality PB, 978-1-59473-138-9 **$15.99**

The Workplace and Spirituality: New Perspectives on Research and Practice
Edited by Dr. Joan Marques, Dr. Satinder Dhiman and Dr. Richard King
6 x 9, 256 pp, HC, 978-1-59473-260-7 **$29.99**

Sacred Texts—SkyLight Illuminations Series

Offers today's spiritual seeker an enjoyable entry into the great classic texts of the world's spiritual traditions. Each classic is presented in an accessible translation, with facing pages of guided commentary from experts, giving you the keys you need to understand the history, context and meaning of the text.

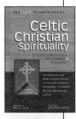

CHRISTIANITY

Celtic Christian Spirituality: Essential Writings—Annotated & Explained
Annotation by Mary C. Earle; Foreword by John Philip Newell
Explores how the writings of this lively tradition embody the gospel.
5½ x 8½, 176 pp (est), Quality PB, 978-1-59473-302-4 **$16.99**

The End of Days: Essential Selections from Apocalyptic Texts—
Annotated & Explained *Annotation by Robert G. Clouse, PhD*
Helps you understand the complex Christian visions of the end of the world.
5½ x 8½, 224 pp, Quality PB, 978-1-59473-170-9 **$16.99**

The Hidden Gospel of Matthew: Annotated & Explained
Translation & Annotation by Ron Miller Discover the words and events that have the strongest connection to the historical Jesus.
5½ x 8½, 272 pp, Quality PB, 978-1-59473-038-2 **$16.99**

The Infancy Gospels of Jesus: Apocryphal Tales from the Childhoods of Mary and Jesus—Annotated & Explained
Translation & Annotation by Stevan Davies; Foreword by A. Edward Siecienski, PhD
A startling presentation of the early lives of Mary, Jesus and other biblical figures that will amuse and surprise you. 5½ x 8½, 176 pp, Quality PB, 978-1-59473-258-4 **$16.99**

The Lost Sayings of Jesus: Teachings from Ancient Christian, Jewish, Gnostic and Islamic Sources—Annotated & Explained
Translation & Annotation by Andrew Phillip Smith; Foreword by Stephan A. Hoeller
This collection of more than three hundred sayings depicts Jesus as a Wisdom teacher who speaks to people of all faiths as a mystic and spiritual master.
5½ x 8½, 240 pp, Quality PB, 978-1-59473-172-3 **$16.99**

Philokalia: The Eastern Christian Spiritual Texts—Selections Annotated & Explained *Annotation by Allyne Smith; Translation by G. E. H. Palmer, Phillip Sherrard and Bishop Kallistos Ware*
The first approachable introduction to the wisdom of the Philokalia, the classic text of Eastern Christian spirituality. 5½ x 8½, 240 pp, Quality PB, 978-1-59473-103-7 **$16.99**

The Sacred Writings of Paul: Selections Annotated & Explained
Translation & Annotation by Ron Miller Leads you into the exciting immediacy of Paul's teachings. 5½ x 8½, 224 pp, Quality PB, 978-1-59473-213-3 **$16.99**

Saint Augustine of Hippo: Selections from *Confessions* and Other Essential Writings—Annotated & Explained
Annotation by Joseph T. Kelley, PhD; Translation by the Augustinian Heritage Institute
Provides insight into the mind and heart of this foundational Christian figure.
5½ x 8½, 272 pp, Quality PB, 978-1-59473-282-9 **$16.99**

St. Ignatius Loyola—The Spiritual Writings: Selections Annotated & Explained *Annotation by Mark Mossa, SJ*
Draws from contemporary translations of original texts focusing on the practical mysticism of Ignatius of Loyola. 5½ x 8½, 224 pp (est), Quality PB, 978-1-59473-301-7 **$16.99**

Sex Texts from the Bible: Selections Annotated & Explained
Translation & Annotation by Teresa J. Hornsby; Foreword by Amy-Jill Levine
Demystifies the Bible's ideas on gender roles, marriage, sexual orientation, virginity, lust and sexual pleasure. 5½ x 8½, 208 pp, Quality PB, 978-1-59473-217-1 **$16.99**

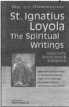

Sacred Texts—continued

ISLAM

Ghazali on the Principles of Islamic Spirituality
Selections from *Forty Foundations of Religion*—Annotated & Explained
Translation & Annotation by Aaron Spevack, PhD
Makes the core message of this influential spiritual master relevant to anyone seeking a balanced understanding of Islam.
5½ x 8½, 208 pp (est), Quality PB, 978-1-59473-284-3 **$16.99**

The Qur'an and Sayings of Prophet Muhammad
Selections Annotated & Explained
Annotation by Sohaib N. Sultan; Translation by Yusuf Ali, Revised by Sohaib N. Sultan; Foreword by Jane I. Smith
Presents the foundational wisdom of Islam in an easy-to-use format.
5½ x 8½, 256 pp, Quality PB, 978-1-59473-222-5 **$16.99**

Rumi and Islam: Selections from His Stories, Poems, and Discourses—
Annotated & Explained *Translation & Annotation by Ibrahim Gamard*
Focuses on Rumi's place within the Sufi tradition of Islam, providing insight into the mystical side of the religion.
5½ x 8½, 240 pp, Quality PB, 978-1-59473-002-3 **$15.99**

EASTERN RELIGIONS

The Art of War—Spirituality for Conflict: Annotated & Explained
by Sun Tzu; Annotation by Thomas Huynh; Translation by Thomas Huynh and the Editors at Sonshi.com; Foreword by Marc Benioff; Preface by Thomas Cleary
Highlights principles that encourage a perceptive and spiritual approach to conflict.
5½ x 8½, 256 pp, Quality PB, 978-1-59473-244-7 **$16.99**

Bhagavad Gita: Annotated & Explained
Translation by Shri Purohit Swami; Annotation by Kendra Crossen Burroughs; Foreword by Andrew Harvey
Presents the classic text's teachings—with no previous knowledge of Hinduism required.
5½ x 8½, 192 pp, Quality PB, 978-1-893361-28-7 **$16.95**

Chuang-tzu: The Tao of Perfect Happiness—Selections Annotated & Explained
Translation & Annotation by Livia Kohn, PhD
Presents Taoism's central message of reverence for the "Way" of the natural world.
5½ x 8½, 240 pp, Quality PB, 978-1-59473-296-6 **$16.99**

Confucius, the *Analects:* The Path of the Sage—Selections Annotated &
Explained *Annotation by Rodney L Taylor, PhD; Translation by James Legge, Revised by Rodney L Taylor, PhD* Explores the ethical and spiritual meaning behind the Confucian way of learning and self-cultivation.
5½ x 8½, 176 pp (est), Quality PB, 978-1-59473-306-2 **$16.99**

Dhammapada: Annotated & Explained
Translation by Max Müller, revised by Jack Maguire; Annotation by Jack Maguire; Foreword by Andrew Harvey Contains all of Buddhism's key teachings, plus commentary that explains all the names, terms and references.
5½ x 8½, 160 pp, b/w photos, Quality PB, 978-1-893361-42-3 **$14.95**

Selections from the Gospel of Sri Ramakrishna: Annotated & Explained
Translation by Swami Nikhilananda; Annotation by Kendra Crossen Burroughs; Foreword by Andrew Harvey Introduces the fascinating world of the Indian mystic and the universal appeal of his message.
5½ x 8½, 240 pp, b/w photos, Quality PB, 978-1-893361-46-1 **$16.95**

Tao Te Ching: Annotated & Explained
Translation & Annotation by Derek Lin; Foreword by Lama Surya Das
Introduces an Eastern classic in an accessible, poetic and completely original way.
5½ x 8½, 208 pp, Quality PB, 978-1-59473-204-1 **$16.99**

Sacred Texts—continued

MORMONISM

The Book of Mormon: Selections Annotated & Explained
Annotation by Jana Riess; Foreword by Phyllis Tickle Explores the sacred epic that is cherished by more than twelve million members of the LDS church as the keystone of their faith. 5½ x 8½, 272 pp, Quality PB, 978-1-59473-076-4 **$16.99**

NATIVE AMERICAN

Native American Stories of the Sacred: Annotated & Explained
Retold & Annotated by Evan T. Pritchard These teaching tales contain elegantly simple illustrations of time-honored truths. 5½ x 8½, 272 pp, Quality PB, 978-1-59473-112-9 **$16.99**

STOICISM

The Meditations of Marcus Aurelius: Selections Annotated & Explained *Annotation by Russell McNeil, PhD; Translation by George Long, revised by Russell McNeil, PhD* Ancient Stoic wisdom that speaks vibrantly today about life, business, government and spirit. 5½ x 8½, 288 pp, Quality PB, 978-1-59473-236-2 **$16.99**

Hinduism / Vedanta

The Four Yogas: A Guide to the Spiritual Paths of Action, Devotion, Meditation and Knowledge *by Swami Adiswarananda*
6 x 9, 320 pp, Quality PB, 978-1-59473-223-2 **$19.99**; HC, 978-1-59473-143-3 **$29.99**

Meditation & Its Practices: A Definitive Guide to Techniques and Traditions of Meditation in Yoga and Vedanta *by Swami Adiswarananda* 6 x 9, 504 pp, Quality PB, 978-1-59473-105-1 **$24.99**

The Spiritual Quest and the Way of Yoga: The Goal, the Journey and the Milestones *by Swami Adiswarananda* 6 x 9, 288 pp, HC, 978-1-59473-113-6 **$29.99**

Sri Ramakrishna, the Face of Silence
by Swami Nikhilananda and Dhan Gopal Mukerji; Edited with an Introduction by Swami Adiswarananda; Foreword by Dhan Gopal Mukerji II 6 x 9, 352 pp, Quality PB, 978-1-59473-233-1 **$21.99**

Sri Sarada Devi, The Holy Mother: Her Teachings and Conversations
Translated with Notes by Swami Nikhilananda; Edited with an Introduction by Swami Adiswarananda 6 x 9, 288 pp, HC, 978-1-59473-070-2 **$29.99**

The Vedanta Way to Peace and Happiness *by Swami Adiswarananda*
6 x 9, 240 pp, Quality PB, 978-1-59473-180-8 **$18.99**; HC, 978-1-59473-034-4 **$29.99**

Vivekananda, World Teacher: His Teachings on the Spiritual Unity of Humankind
Edited and with an Introduction by Swami Adiswarananda
6 x 9, 272 pp, Quality PB, 978-1-59473-210-2 **$21.99**

Sikhism

The First Sikh Spiritual Master: Timeless Wisdom from the Life and Teachings of Guru Nanak *by Harish Dhillon* 6 x 9, 192 pp, Quality PB, 978-1-59473-209-6 **$16.99**

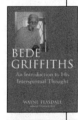

Spiritual Biography

Spiritual Leaders Who Changed the World
The Essential Handbook to the Past Century of Religion
Edited by Ira Rifkin and the Editors at SkyLight Paths; Foreword by Dr. Robert Coles
An invaluable reference to the most important spiritual leaders of the past 100 years.
6 x 9, 304 pp, b/w photos, Quality PB, 978-1-59473-241-6 **$18.99**

Mahatma Gandhi: His Life and Ideas *by Charles F. Andrews; Foreword by Dr. Arun Gandhi* Examines the religious ideas and political dynamics that influenced the birth of the peaceful resistance movement. 6 x 9, 336 pp, b/w photos, Quality PB, 978-1-893361-89-8 **$18.95**

Bede Griffiths: An Introduction to His Interspiritual Thought
by Wayne Teasdale The first study of his contemplative experience and thought, exploring the intersection of Hinduism and Christianity.
6 x 9, 288 pp, Quality PB, 978-1-893361-77-5 **$18.95**

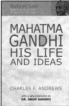

About SKYLIGHT PATHS Publishing

SkyLight Paths Publishing is creating a place where people of different spiritual traditions come together for challenge and inspiration, a place where we can help each other understand the mystery that lies at the heart of our existence.

Through spirituality, our religious beliefs are increasingly becoming a part of our lives—rather than *apart* from our lives. While many of us may be more interested than ever in spiritual growth, we may be less firmly planted in traditional religion. Yet, we do want to deepen our relationship to the sacred, to learn from our own as well as from other faith traditions, and to practice in new ways.

SkyLight Paths sees both believers and seekers as a community that increasingly transcends traditional boundaries of religion and denomination—people wanting to learn from each other, *walking together, finding the way.*

For your information and convenience, at the back of this book we have provided a list of other SkyLight Paths books you might find interesting and useful. They cover the following subjects:

Buddhism / Zen	Global Spiritual	Monasticism
Catholicism	Perspectives	Mysticism
Children's Books	Gnosticism	Poetry
Christianity	Hinduism /	Prayer
Comparative	Vedanta	Religious Etiquette
Religion	Inspiration	Retirement
Current Events	Islam / Sufism	Spiritual Biography
Earth-Based	Judaism	Spiritual Direction
Spirituality	Kabbalah	Spirituality
Enneagram	Meditation	Women's Interest
	Midrash Fiction	Worship

Or phone, fax, mail or e-mail to: SKYLIGHT PATHS Publishing
Sunset Farm Offices, Route 4 • P.O. Box 237 • Woodstock, Vermont 05091
Tel: (802) 457-4000 • Fax: (802) 457-4004 • www.skylightpaths.com
Credit card orders: (800) 962-4544 (8:30AM–5:30PM ET Monday–Friday)
Generous discounts on quantity orders. SATISFACTION GUARANTEED. Prices subject to change.